Personal Bible Study Notebook Volume 2

John C. Souter

Tyndale House Publishers, Inc.
Wheaton, Illinois

Coverdale House Publishers Ltd.
London, England

PERSONAL BIBLE STUDY NOTEBOOK VOLUME TWO

ISBN 8423-4818-2

Copyright © 1973, 1976 by John C. Souter

Personal Bible Study Notebook was originally published by World Thrust Inc. Volume II is published by Tyndale House Publishers, Inc. with permission of World Thrust Inc. All rights reserved. No portion of this book may be used in any form without the written permission of the author or the publishers, with the exception of brief excerpts in magazine articles, reviews, etc.

First printing, January 1976

Printed in United States of America

Contents

Introduction 4
List of Methods 4
1. The Importance Of The Bible 5
2. Why Study The Bible? 6
3. How To Develop The Bible Study Habit 7
4. Some Secrets For Success 8
5. Bibles And Reference Books 10
6. What's In The Bible? 11
7. How To Use The Methods 13
8. What To Study 18
Daily Log 22
The Methods
   Verse Glance 28-38
   Proverbs Glance 39-48
   Meditation 49-58
   Psalm Glance 59-68
   Paragraph Glance 69-88
   Prophecy Glance 89-108
   Paraphrase 109-118
   Law Study 119-128
   Prophecy Study 129-138
   Epistle Study 139-148
   The Five W's 149-158
   Teachings of Jesus 159-168
   Biography Study 169-178
   Book Study 179-188

Introduction

The *Personal Bible Study Notebook* is a tool designed to help you dig into God's Word. It was created for Christians like you, who want to study the Bible, but just don't know where to begin. This notebook contains everything you need to develop deep, meaningful, and consistent Bible study. Here's what this notebook will do for you:

- Provide study material for every day in the year
- Present 14 different ways to study the Bible
- Offer daily variety
- Record what is learned for future reference
- Introduce you to every part of Scripture
- Teach both Bible facts and principles
- Help you apply Scripture to everyday life

List of Methods

The Daily Log

5-MINUTE METHODS
1) Verse Glance
2) Proverbs Glance
3) Meditation
4) Psalm Glance
5) Paragraph Glance
6) Prophecy Glance
7) Paraphrase

15-MINUTE METHODS
8) Law Study
9) Prophecy Study
10) Epistle Study
11) The Five W's
12) Teachings of Jesus

30-MINUTE METHODS
13) Biography Study
14) Book Study

1

The Importance Of The Bible

Who but God could have written a book over a period of 2,000 years, in three different languages, on three continents, by at least 37 individual authors, in 66 parts, and come up with the most significant Book in history? The Bible is not merely *a* book, it is *the Book*, the Book that from the importance of its subjects, the wideness of its range, and the majesty of its Author stands as high above all other books as the heaven is above the earth.

Although the Bible is thousands of years old and deals with many subjects far ahead of the era in which it was written, it is medically, scientifically, prophetically, psychologically, and historically accurate. No other book has inspired so many other books or so much poetry or so much art. No other book has changed so many lives.

We are told that the Bible is capable of looking into our hearts and discerning what is good and what is bad. It is alive. It is constantly active on God's behalf. It is able to teach us what we need to know to live a happy life. It is able to separate us, correct us, feed us, and show us how to develop a God-like personality. In short, the Bible has what we need.

Have you learned to tap the wisdom in this Book? Has it become the most important Book in your life? You can discover the unbelievable riches in the Bible for yourself. God wrote this Book for you — so that you might live a better life.

Why Study The Bible?

Some people hold that the Bible should be read like any other book. The problem is that the Bible is not like any other book and cannot be treated as such. There is simply no easy way to read it.

God uses some interesting words to describe what He wants us to do with His Book. He says we are to abide in, delight in, look intently at, meditate in, chew, observe, and love His laws. Each of us is told "Study to show thyself approved unto God, a workman that needeth not to be ashamed, rightly dividing the word of truth." (II Timothy 2:15 KJV). God wants us to study the Bible.

Bible study brings special rewards from God. He says in James 1:25 that anyone who looks intently on the Word and lives by it will be blessed in what he does. He tells us in Psalms (1:2-6) that meditation on His Word will bring prosperity in whatever we do. We will become wiser than our enemies (119:98), develop more insight than all our teachers (119:99), and understand more than the aged (119:100) because we have learned to study and apply God's laws for living.

Getting to know the God of the Book, learning to live with yourself, and leading a happy life are just some of the benefits from time spent in Scripture. When you become involved in meaningful Bible study, you will never again be satisfied with a casual reading of His Book. Come face to face with spiritual discovery and you will want to make it an everyday experience. The more you come to know God, the more exciting your own personal Bible study will become.

3
How To Develop The Bible Study Habit

For years I studied the Bible on a sporadic basis. I tried hard — but something always interfered until I would realize that I hadn't been in the Book for weeks. Not until I was challenged to commit at least five minutes a day to God did I find regularity in my daily spiritual life. I made a life-long vow to give God five minutes of Bible study time each day.

This was not a casual decision, because Scripture contains a clear warning. "When you make a vow to God, do not be late in paying it, for He takes no delight in fools. Pay what you vow! It is better that you should not vow than that you should vow and not pay." (Ecclesiastes 5:4-5 NASV).

Sometimes we forget that God promises to be our power to do what He commands us to do. "(Not in your own strength) for it is God Who is all the while effectually at work in you — energizing and creating in you the power and desire — both to will and to work for His good pleasure and satisfaction and delight." (Philippians 2:13 Amplified Bible).

I asked God to give me the discipline needed to fulfill this vow consistently. When I made this study time the most important portion of my schedule, He gave me daily success. When I built my day around this activity, I achieved Bible study regularity — for the first time in my life.

Think seriously about making this vow. The importance of a vow tends to create in you a strong desire to keep your promise to God. Spending five minutes a day in God's Word will not only add vitality to your spiritual life, but will improve living in general.

Some Secrets For Success

Here are a few hints to make your Bible study more effective.

Before you begin the study of God's Book, ask Him to unlock His storehouse of wisdom and knowledge. Expect blessings from God every time you sit down to study. No quiet time is ever complete until you have found something which you can apply to your personal life. Like Jacob, when he wrestled with the angel of the Lord, say, "I will not let Thee go except Thou bless me." (Genesis 32:26 KJV).

Set a definite time for Bible study. It is much easier to remember to study when it is part of your daily routine. On weekends a different time may have to be scheduled because of your change of routine. Because some people can concentrate better in the morning, and others think more clearly in the evening, you should select your best time of day for study.

Each method is given a minimum time limit. You can select a 5-minute, 15-minute, or 30-minute method for study, but always plan to spend at least the suggested time for the method you select. However, if you find yourself studying past this limit when exciting discoveries are made – don't be surprised. If you work fast, you will find that this helps your concentration; so learn to be quick and efficient.

There are days when you won't feel like studying or when no time will be available. When this happens, choose a short five-minute method. Missing one day will make it easy to miss the next; so discipline yourself to do at least one method every day. The Daily Log will help you check your study regularity.

Choose a place where you will not be interrupted, one that allows room for both your Bible and *Personal Bible Study Notebook*. If possible, use the same place every day.

It has been proven that we remember more when we write things down. Each method in this notebook requires you to record your spiritual discoveries. When you read these studies later, the full message will be rekindled in your mind. When you've finished a notebook, you can remove the methods and file them by subject matter. In this way you will have background for Sunday school lessons and devotionals.

Don't expect answers for every question in every method. Although the questions are general, they will not all apply to every passage. When a question does not have an answer, write "NA" (not applicable) and move on.

Try to answer all the questions without the aid of a commentary. It is exciting to discover nuggets of truth for yourself, and these spiritual gems help to make studying God's Book an adventure. Use a Bible dictionary or commentary only after you have exhausted the information you can find in Scripture itself.

Study as many different Bible passages as possible; don't ignore any portion of God's Word. You can receive spiritual food from every passage.

Always ask yourself why God caused each passage to be written. Although He deals with men differently in different ages, His basic nature does not change. Look beyond the obvious message of each passage to see the basic, unchangeable principles which run throughout Scripture. When you know what God is trying to accomplish as a whole, you will better understand the portion of Scripture you are studying.

5

Bibles And Reference Books

The Bible was originally written in Greek, Hebrew, and Aramaic. Over the years many different translations have been made. Because not all translations accurately express the meaning of the original languages, it is important to purchase a Bible which is both accurate and readable. One of the best translations for study purposes is the *New American Standard Bible*.

Your Bible should contain cross-references which will lead you to other Scripture passages which are similar to the one you are studying. It is important to remember, however, that cross-references are not inspired by God and *never* list all of the Scripture passages that are related to the portion you are studying.

For inspiration and stimulation, paraphrases like the *Living Bible* are excellent and may be used effectively for methods like Meditation. The *Amplified Bible* reveals the expanded meaning behind Bible words and phrases.

Two books which you will find essential to deep Bible study are a good Bible dictionary and a complete concordance. *Zondervan's Pictorial Bible Dictionary*, is an excellent aid for background material, much of which is not found in Scripture itself. *Young's Analytical Concordance to the Bible* is also a very effective tool if used correctly. To find a verse containing the word "love", you would first look up the word in alphabetical order. In the Greek language there are several words translated as "love", each with a different meaning. If you wanted to find the type of love recorded in John 3:16, you would look under each type of love listed until you came to the listing for John 3:16. In this case, it would be listed under agapao (Godly love).

6

What's In The Bible?

The Bible is not really one Book, but a collection of many books, prophecies, poems, and letters. To be able to study the Bible you must know what it is like. Because each section of Scripture was written for a different purpose, each must be studied differently. Here is a brief description of the major types of Bible passages:

The Law — The books of Hebrew Law are found exclusively in the Old Testament and contain three types of regulations. The *moral law* contained in the ten commandments set the boundary for right and wrong. The *political regulations* were Israel's criminal law. The *religious rules* governed the purity of worship, the sanctuary, and the priesthood. These laws, although lengthy and repetitious, form the hardrock foundation for the rest of the Bible. No Christian can develop a complete knowledge of the Bible without exposure to these books.

Historical Books — These are the Bible books which tell us of early man, the nation of Israel, the Jews, the life of Christ, and the New Testament Church. These books contain accounts of real people with real problems and tell us a lot about how God wants us to behave.

Poetry Books — The poetry contained in Bible books is unlike the modern poetry with which we are familiar. Much of its form has been lost through translation and it does not rhyme. Originally many of these poems were composed as songs. Some of the strong themes in Biblical poetry are God's goodness, man's need for divine help, and wisdom versus foolishness.

The Prophets — These books contain God's revelation of the future. Almost all of these books are in the Old Testament and contain prophecy that was designed to make Israel repent of her idolatry, as well as many long-range prophecies which predict God's master plan for the world.

The Gospels — Since the time of Christ, the words and images recorded in the Gospels have left a permanent mark on the hearts of men. These four books contain the historical record of Jesus Christ's earthly life and His revolutionary teachings about the Kingdom of God.

The Epistles — Each of the epistles was originally a letter written to a New Testament church or to a first-century believer. While they do contain personal information, they are primarily practical teachings of Christian living.

THE LAW	POETRY	THE GOSPELS
Exodus	Job	Matthew
Leviticus	Psalms	Mark
Numbers	Proverbs	Luke
Deuteronomy	Ecclesiastes	John
HISTORY	Song of Solomon	**THE EPISTLES**
Genesis	**THE PROPHETS**	Romans
Exodus	Isaiah	I Corinthians
Numbers	Jeremiah	II Corinthians
Joshua	Lamentations	Galatians
Judges	Ezekiel	Ephesians
Ruth	Daniel	Philippians
I Samuel	Hosea	Colossians
II Samuel	Joel	I Thessalonians
I Kings	Amos	II Thessalonians
II Kings	Obadiah	I Timothy
I Chronicles	Jonah	II Timothy
II Chronicles	Micah	Titus
Ezra	Nahum	Philemon
Nehemiah	Habakkuk	Hebrews
Esther	Zephaniah	James
Matthew	Haggai	I Peter
Mark	Zechariah	II Peter
Luke	Malachi	I John
John	Revelation	II John
Acts		III John
		Jude

It must be remembered that any book may contain many different types of passages. For example, many historical books contain prophetic or poetical passages. Some of the poetry books contain prophetic and historical information. Chapter seven has a list of methods that can be used to study each type of passage described above.

7

How To Use The Methods

The Daily Log
Purpose — To check your daily Bible study faithfulness.
How To Begin — Each day after a Bible study is completed, put the name of the method you used opposite the current day of the month. After two months, check both your consistency and variety in the studies used.

5-MINUTE METHODS

1) Verse Glance
Purpose — To receive concentrated Bible truth quickly from one important verse.
How To Begin — Select a verse which has a clear message. As you answer each question, try to understand what God is teaching.

2) Proverbs Glance
Purpose — To expose the meaning of a single proverb and apply God's principles for living.
How To Begin — Choose a proverb which teaches practical information. Find God's basic, underlying principle of life contained in this proverb. Make your answers as personal as possible.

3) Meditation
Purpose — To contemplate a portion of God's Word for a whole day.
How To Begin — Carefully read the passage selected, examining each phrase. Choose one important verse to meditate on during the day. Practice applying its principles moment by moment.

4) Psalm Glance
Purpose — To survey quickly the contents of one Psalm.
How To Begin — Skim the contents of a Psalm; then quickly answer the questions. The "type" of Psalm labels what it is about.

5) Paragraph Glance
Purpose — To record the contents of a Bible book in a day-by-day study.
How To Begin — Choose a Bible book. (Use a Bible translation that indicates paragraph divisions, but which does not give a paragraph summary). Write the references for each paragraph on the left hand side of the line. Write a summary of the paragraph contents on the right of the line.

6) Prophecy Glance
Purpose — To summarize a prophecy book in a day-by-day study.
How To Begin — Select a prophecy book. Write the reference for each natural passage division (by paragraphs) on the left and a summary of any prophecy it contains on the right. Put a large "P" opposite each paragraph that is actually predictive. It will take two or three sheets to complete a single prophecy book.

7) Paraphrase
Purpose — To be able to understand a short Bible message by putting it into your own words.
How To Begin — Read the passage you have selected in two different translations (do NOT use a Bible paraphrase). Write the passage in your own words but stay as close to the meaning of the original as possible.

15-MINUTE METHODS

8) Law Study
Purpose — To expose the original meaning of the Jewish Laws and apply them to your personal life.
How To Begin — Select a passage and look for its 20th-century application. Locate New Testament passages which teach the same principle, using cross-references and your concordance.

9) Prophecy Study
Purpose — To reveal the purpose and meaning of one prophecy.
How To Begin — Make sure that you select a passage which foretells some event (Prophecy Glance can help you here). Always look for two fulfillments, one near, and one far from the date the passage was written. If you have difficulty interpreting the symbolism in the prophecy, look it up in a Bible commentary.

10) Epistle Study
Purpose — To examine in depth a section of a New Testament letter,
How To Begin — Select a shorter passage to allow you to dig in deeply. It may be any combination of four passage types: *doctrinal*, which gives basic Christian teachings; *instructional*, which tells the reader how to live; *personal*, which deals with the author's personal business; and *correctional*, which takes care of some problem. Over successive days you may want to study a complete chapter or book.

11) The Five W's
Purpose — To expose the important facts in a history section.
How To Begin — Locate the five W's, (who, when, where, what and why) by developing a reporter's eye. Look for the clues within the narrative which give these facts. Often they will be hidden under

the surface and must be extracted from circumstantial information. Determine why the event was allowed to take place.

12) Teachings of Jesus
Purpose — To understand the full meaning of what Jesus taught.
How To Begin — Select a passage in the Gospels which contains a message or parable from Jesus. Look for the basic, underlying principle He is teaching and apply it to your life.

30-MINUTE METHODS
13) Biography Study
Purpose — To learn the spiritual reasons behind a character's existence in the sacred Record.
How To Begin — Select a Bible character. A complete concordance will show all of the passages where his name is found. For major characters, much reading will be necessary. As you read, keep your eyes open for information which will answer the questions. Put verse references with each answer you find so the facts can be located in later studies.

14) Book Study
Purpose — To understand the basic content, background, and purpose of a Bible book.
How To Begin — Select a book and answer all of the questions from the book itself. Most of the background material is located in the first and last chapters (and verses) of the book. Cross-references should take you to other passages which contain background information. When you have exhausted these avenues of study, consult a Bible dictionary to complete your knowledge. Here you will find an outline of the book and additional Scripture passages for background information.

Which Method To Use

In chapter eight you will find a list of suggested Bible passages to study with every method in this book. However, if you have a passage you want to study and don't know which method to use on it, you can select an appropriate method by using the short guide below.

        The Law Books
           Law Study (15)
           Paragraph Glance (5)
           The Five W's (15)
        The Historical Books
           The Five W's (15)
           Biography Study (30)
           Paragraph Glance (5)

The Poetry Books
　　Psalm Glance (5)
　　Proverbs Glance (5)
　　Paraphrase (5)
The Prophetic Books
　　Prophecy Glance (5)
　　Prophecy Study (15)
The Gospels
　　Teachings of Jesus (15)
　　The Five W's (15)
　　Biography Study (30)
　　Paragraph Glance (5)
The Epistles
　　Epistle Study (15)
　　Paraphrase (5)
　　Meditation (5)
　　Verse Glance (5)
　　Paragraph Glance (5)
For Devotional Studies
　　Verse Glance (5)
　　Proverbs Glance (5)
　　Meditation (5)
　　Psalm Glance (5)
　　Paraphrase (5)

What To Study

This chapter contains some suggested study passages selected carefully to introduce you to the different parts of God's Word. Check off each passage as you study it. If you are not familiar with the contents of the Bible, you might like to begin with survey methods like Paragraph and Prophecy Glance.

1) **Verse Glance**
   - ☐ Ephesians 4:31
   - ☐ John 5:24
   - ☐ Jeremiah 33:3
   - ☐ Luke 12:22, 23
   - ☐ Ephesians 2:10
   - ☐ Jeremiah 17:9, 10
   - ☐ Philippians 2:3, 4
   - ☐ Romans 1:18, 19
   - ☐ I Corinthians 6:20
   - ☐ I John 3:14
   - ☐ Galatians 5:16, 17
   - ☐ Ephesians 4:28
   - ☐ Romans 8:28, 29
   - ☐ Galatians 6:3
   - ☐ Ecclesiastes 5:8
   - ☐ Isaiah 5:20, 21
   - ☐ II Corinthians 10:5
   - ☐ II Corinthians 4:16
   - ☐ Acts 4:12
   - ☐ II Corinthians 13:5

2) **Proverbs Glance**
   - ☐ Proverbs 21:13
   - ☐ Proverbs 26:24–26
   - ☐ Proverbs 19:15
   - ☐ Proverbs 19:2
   - ☐ Proverbs 1:24–30
   - ☐ Proverbs 22:29
   - ☐ Proverbs 14:6
   - ☐ Proverbs 24:21
   - ☐ Proverbs 23:12
   - ☐ Proverbs 19:26
   - ☐ Proverbs 22:17–21
   - ☐ Proverbs 28:24
   - ☐ Proverbs 15:10
   - ☐ Proverbs 15:8
   - ☐ Proverbs 18:2
   - ☐ Proverbs 11:2
   - ☐ Proverbs 14:29
   - ☐ Proverbs 15:22
   - ☐ Proverbs 17:27
   - ☐ Proverbs 19:13

3) **Meditation**
   - ☐ James 2:14–26
   - ☐ Proverbs 7:6–23
   - ☐ Numbers 14:1–25
   - ☐ Luke 11:1–13
   - ☐ II Peter 1:1–11
   - ☐ Mark 12:1–12
   - ☐ Luke 11:42–54
   - ☐ Revelation 1:1–8
   - ☐ II Samuel 18:1–18
   - ☐ II Samuel 18:19–33
   - ☐ Galatians 5:16–26
   - ☐ John 1:1–18
   - ☐ Revelation 21:1–27
   - ☐ Job 26:1–14
   - ☐ Job 40:1–24
   - ☐ II Chronicles 1:1–17
   - ☐ I Kings 17:1–24
   - ☐ Luke 13:10–17
   - ☐ Judges 6:7–32
   - ☐ Judges 6:33–7:25

- ☐ Acts 21:1–16
- ☐ Acts 21:17–36
- ☐ Acts 21:37–22:29
- ☐ Luke 3:1–20
- ☐ Matthew 22:1–14

4) **Psalm Glance**
- ☐ Psalm 104
- ☐ Psalm 51
- ☐ Psalm 119:1–8
- ☐ Psalm 119:97–104
- ☐ Psalm 119:105–112
- ☐ Psalm 124
- ☐ Psalm 98
- ☐ Psalm 84
- ☐ Psalm 128
- ☐ Psalm 95

5) **Paragraph Glance**
- ☐ Galatians 1
- ☐ Galatians 2
- ☐ Galatians 3
- ☐ Galatians 4
- ☐ Galatians 5
- ☐ Galatians 6
- ☐ Mark 1
- ☐ Mark 2
- ☐ Mark 3
- ☐ Mark 4
- ☐ Mark 5
- ☐ Mark 6
- ☐ Mark 7
- ☐ Mark 8
- ☐ Mark 9

6) **Prophecy Glance**
- ☐ Daniel 7
- ☐ Daniel 8
- ☐ Daniel 9
- ☐ Daniel 10
- ☐ Daniel 11
- ☐ Daniel 12
- ☐ Joel 1
- ☐ Joel 2
- ☐ Joel 3
- ☐ Isaiah 1
- ☐ Isaiah 2
- ☐ Isaiah 3

- ☐ Judges 8:1–35
- ☐ Judges 13:1–25
- ☐ Judges 14:1–20
- ☐ Judges 15:1–20
- ☐ Judges 16:1–31

- ☐ Psalm 11
- ☐ Psalm 100
- ☐ Psalm 104
- ☐ Psalm 6
- ☐ Psalm 144
- ☐ Psalm 73
- ☐ Psalm 9
- ☐ Psalm 62
- ☐ Psalm 119:9–16
- ☐ Psalm 148

- ☐ Mark 10
- ☐ Mark 11
- ☐ Mark 12
- ☐ Mark 13
- ☐ Mark 14
- ☐ I Samuel 1
- ☐ I Samuel 2
- ☐ I Samuel 3
- ☐ I Samuel 4
- ☐ I Samuel 5
- ☐ I Samuel 6
- ☐ I Samuel 7
- ☐ I Samuel 8
- ☐ I Samuel 9
- ☐ I Samuel 10

- ☐ Isaiah 7
- ☐ Isaiah 8
- ☐ Isaiah 9
- ☐ Isaiah 10
- ☐ Isaiah 11
- ☐ Isaiah 12
- ☐ Jeremiah 1
- ☐ Jeremiah 2
- ☐ Jeremiah 3
- ☐ Jeremiah 4
- ☐ Jeremiah 5
- ☐ Jeremiah 6

- [ ] Isaiah 4
- [ ] Isaiah 5
- [ ] Isaiah 6
- [ ] Jeremiah 7
- [ ] Jeremiah 8
- [ ] Jeremiah 9

7) **Paraphrase**
- [ ] Romans 3:24, 25
- [ ] I John 3:17, 18
- [ ] II Peter 1:10, 11
- [ ] Hebrews 12:11
- [ ] I Peter 2:20, 21
- [ ] Romans 8:2, 3
- [ ] I Timothy 1:15, 16
- [ ] Ephesians 1:7–9
- [ ] Galatians 6:7–9
- [ ] Colossians 2:8–10
- [ ] I Timothy 6:6–9
- [ ] Philippians 2:14, 15
- [ ] James 3:16–18
- [ ] Hebrews 12:14, 15
- [ ] I Peter 3:8, 9
- [ ] James 5:7–9
- [ ] Titus 1:15, 16
- [ ] II Corinthians 9:6, 7
- [ ] I Corinthians 13:4–7
- [ ] Romans 6:16–18

8) **Law Study**
- [ ] Leviticus 17:10–16
- [ ] Exodus 22:28–31
- [ ] Deuteronomy 14:22–27
- [ ] Leviticus 16:29–34
- [ ] Exodus 21:1–6
- [ ] Exodus 20:8–12
- [ ] Exodus 20:13–17
- [ ] Deuteronomy 20:19, 20
- [ ] Deuteronomy 22:1–4
- [ ] Deuteronomy 11:8–12

9) **Prophecy Study**
- [ ] Isaiah 49:1–7
- [ ] Matthew 24:15–27
- [ ] Isaiah 11:1–9
- [ ] I Thessalonians 4:13–18
- [ ] Revelation 13:11–18
- [ ] Daniel 9:24–27
- [ ] Daniel 11:40–45
- [ ] Revelation 11:1–13
- [ ] II Thessalonians 2:1–12
- [ ] Zechariah 3:6–10

10) **Epistle Study**
- [ ] II John 1–13
- [ ] I Peter 5:1–5
- [ ] I Peter 5:6–11
- [ ] Hebrews 12:1–13
- [ ] Philippians 4:10–19
- [ ] Ephesians 6:1–4
- [ ] II Corinthians 8:16–23
- [ ] I Corinthians 3:10–15
- [ ] Romans 12:3–8
- [ ] Romans 14:1–12

11) **The Five W's**
- [ ] Acts 17:16–34
- [ ] Mark 12:41–44
- [ ] John 20:1–10
- [ ] Acts 12:1–17
- [ ] I Kings 17:1–7
- [ ] Esther 1:10–22
- [ ] Acts 4:1–22
- [ ] Acts 21:7–14
- [ ] Exodus 1:8–14
- [ ] Joshua 10:6–11

12) **Teachings of Jesus**
- [ ] Matthew 13:47–50
- [ ] Luke 9:23–27
- [ ] Mark 4:21–25
- [ ] Matthew 18:21–35
- [ ] John 6:41–51
- [ ] John 12:44–50
- [ ] Mark 12:28–34
- [ ] Matthew 5:38–42
- [ ] Luke 20:9–18
- [ ] Luke 12:35–40

13) **Biography Study**
    - [ ] Philip (Acts 6:5, 8:5ff., 21:8)
    - [ ] Ruth (Book of Ruth)
    - [ ] John Mark (Acts 12:12, 25; 13:5, 13; 15:36–41; 2 Tim. 4:11)
    - [ ] Caleb (Num. 13:6, 30ff.)
    - [ ] Mary Magdalene (Luke 8:2; Matt 27:56ff.; John 19:25ff.)

14) **Book Study**
    - [ ] John
    - [ ] Jude
    - [ ] Joshua
    - [ ] Zechariah
    - [ ] I Peter

What To Do Each Day

Each day as you study you will want to do the following three things:

1) Select a passage and method from chapter eight.
2) Record the method you are using in the Daily Log.
3) Study the passage you have selected.

Daily Log

"... they received the word with great eagerness, examining the Scriptures daily, to see whether these things were so."   *Acts 17:11b NASV*

Each day you study God's Word, list the name of the method used opposite the correct day. In this way you can tell how faithful you have been.

Month_____ Year _____

1_____	22_____	11_____
2_____	23_____	12_____
3_____	24_____	13_____
4_____	25_____	14_____
5_____	26_____	15_____
6_____	27_____	16_____
7_____	28_____	17_____
8_____	29_____	18_____
9_____	30_____	19_____
10_____	31_____	20_____
11_____	Month_____	21_____
12_____	1_____	22_____
13_____	2_____	23_____
14_____	3_____	24_____
15_____	4_____	25_____
16_____	5_____	26_____
17_____	6_____	27_____
18_____	7_____	28_____
19_____	8_____	29_____
20_____	9_____	30_____
21_____	10_____	31_____

Daily Log

"... they received the word with great eagerness, examining the Scriptures daily, to see whether these things were so."   *Acts 17:11b NASV*

Each day you study God's Word, list the name of the method used opposite the correct day. In this way you can tell how faithful you have been.

Month_____ Year_____

1_____	22_____	11_____
2_____	23_____	12_____
3_____	24_____	13_____
4_____	25_____	14_____
5_____	26_____	15_____
6_____	27_____	16_____
7_____	28_____	17_____
8_____	29_____	18_____
9_____	30_____	19_____
10_____	31_____	20_____
11_____	Month_____	21_____
12_____	1_____	22_____
13_____	2_____	23_____
14_____	3_____	24_____
15_____	4_____	25_____
16_____	5_____	26_____
17_____	6_____	27_____
18_____	7_____	28_____
19_____	8_____	29_____
20_____	9_____	30_____
21_____	10_____	31_____

Daily Log

"... they received the word with great eagerness, examining the Scriptures daily, to see whether these things were so." Acts 17:11b NASV

Each day you study God's Word, list the name of the method used opposite the correct day. In this way you can tell how faithful you have been.

Month_____ Year_____

1_____	22_____	11_____
2_____	23_____	12_____
3_____	24_____	13_____
4_____	25_____	14_____
5_____	26_____	15_____
6_____	27_____	16_____
7_____	28_____	17_____
8_____	29_____	18_____
9_____	30_____	19_____
10_____	31_____	20_____
11_____	Month_____	21_____
12_____	1_____	22_____
13_____	2_____	23_____
14_____	3_____	24_____
15_____	4_____	25_____
16_____	5_____	26_____
17_____	6_____	27_____
18_____	7_____	28_____
19_____	8_____	29_____
20_____	9_____	30_____
21_____	10_____	31_____

Daily Log

"... they received the word with great eagerness, examining the Scriptures daily, to see whether these things were so."   Acts 17:11b NASV

Each day you study God's Word, list the name of the method used opposite the correct day. In this way you can tell how faithful you have been.

Month_____ Year _____

1_____ 22 _____ 11 _____
2_____ 23 _____ 12 _____
3_____ 24 _____ 13 _____
4_____ 25 _____ 14 _____
5_____ 26 _____ 15 _____
6_____ 27 _____ 16 _____
7_____ 28 _____ 17 _____
8_____ 29 _____ 18 _____
9_____ 30 _____ 19 _____
10_____ 31 _____ 20 _____
11_____ Month _____ 21 _____
12_____ 1 _____ 22 _____
13_____ 2 _____ 23 _____
14_____ 3 _____ 24 _____
15_____ 4 _____ 25 _____
16_____ 5 _____ 26 _____
17_____ 6 _____ 27 _____
18_____ 7 _____ 28 _____
19_____ 8 _____ 29 _____
20_____ 9 _____ 30 _____
21_____ 10 _____ 31 _____

Daily Log

"... they received the word with great eagerness, examining the Scriptures daily, to see whether these things were so."   *Acts 17:11b NASV*

Each day you study God's Word, list the name of the method used opposite the correct day. In this way you can tell how faithful you have been.

Month_____ Year_____

1_____	22_____	11_____
2_____	23_____	12_____
3_____	24_____	13_____
4_____	25_____	14_____
5_____	26_____	15_____
6_____	27_____	16_____
7_____	28_____	17_____
8_____	29_____	18_____
9_____	30_____	19_____
10_____	31_____	20_____
11_____	Month_____	21_____
12_____	1_____	22_____
13_____	2_____	23_____
14_____	3_____	24_____
15_____	4_____	25_____
16_____	5_____	26_____
17_____	6_____	27_____
18_____	7_____	28_____
19_____	8_____	29_____
20_____	9_____	30_____
21_____	10_____	31_____

Daily Log

"... they received the word with great eagerness, examining the Scriptures daily, to see whether these things were so."   Acts 17:11b NASV

Each day you study God's Word, list the name of the method used opposite the correct day. In this way you can tell how faithful you have been.

Month_____ Year_____

1_____	22_____	11_____
2_____	23_____	12_____
3_____	24_____	13_____
4_____	25_____	14_____
5_____	26_____	15_____
6_____	27_____	16_____
7_____	28_____	17_____
8_____	29_____	18_____
9_____	30_____	19_____
10_____	31_____	20_____
11_____	Month_____	21_____
12_____	1_____	22_____
13_____	2_____	23_____
14_____	3_____	24_____
15_____	4_____	25_____
16_____	5_____	26_____
17_____	6_____	27_____
18_____	7_____	28_____
19_____	8_____	29_____
20_____	9_____	30_____
21_____	10_____	31_____

Verse Glance   5 min.

Verse Selected_____ Date_____
1. List any action verbs found in this verse._____
_____
2. What or who is doing the action?_____
_____
3. What is the central message of this verse?_____
_____
_____
4. Are any promises or blessings given?_____
_____
_____
5. Do I reflect the message of this verse?_____
_____
_____

Verse Selected_____ Date_____
1. List any action verbs found in this verse._____
_____
2. What or who is doing the action?_____
_____
3. What is the central message of this verse?_____
_____
_____
4. Are any promises or blessings given?_____
_____
_____
5. Do I reflect the message of this verse?_____
_____
_____

©1973, John C. Souter. Not to be reproduced.

Verse Glance   *5 min.*

Verse Selected_____ Date_____

1. List any action verbs found in this verse._____
   _____

2. What or who is doing the action?_____
   _____

3. What is the central message of this verse?_____
   _____
   _____

4. Are any promises or blessings given?_____
   _____
   _____

5. Do I reflect the message of this verse?_____
   _____
   _____

Verse Selected_____ Date_____

1. List any action verbs found in this verse._____
   _____

2. What or who is doing the action?_____
   _____

3. What is the central message of this verse?_____
   _____
   _____

4. Are any promises or blessings given?_____
   _____
   _____

5. Do I reflect the message of this verse?_____
   _____
   _____

©1973, John C. Souter. Not to be reproduced.

Verse Glance 5 min.

Verse Selected_____ Date_____

1. List any action verbs found in this verse._____
   _____

2. What or who is doing the action?_____
   _____

3. What is the central message of this verse?_____
   _____
   _____

4. Are any promises or blessings given?_____
   _____
   _____

5. Do I reflect the message of this verse?_____
   _____
   _____

Verse Selected_____ Date_____

1. List any action verbs found in this verse._____
   _____

2. What or who is doing the action?_____
   _____

3. What is the central message of this verse?_____
   _____
   _____

4. Are any promises or blessings given?_____
   _____
   _____

5. Do I reflect the message of this verse?_____
   _____
   _____

©1973, John C. Souter. Not to be reproduced.

Verse Glance   5 min.

Verse Selected_____Date_____
1. List any action verbs found in this verse._____
_____

2. What or who is doing the action?_____
_____

3. What is the central message of this verse?_____
_____
_____

4. Are any promises or blessings given?_____
_____
_____

5. Do I reflect the message of this verse?_____
_____
_____

Verse Selected_____Date_____
1. List any action verbs found in this verse._____
_____

2. What or who is doing the action?_____
_____

3. What is the central message of this verse?_____
_____
_____

4. Are any promises or blessings given?_____
_____
_____

5. Do I reflect the message of this verse?_____
_____
_____

©1973, John C. Souter. Not to be reproduced.

Verse Glance   5 min.

Verse Selected_____ Date_____

1. List any action verbs found in this verse._____
   _____

2. What or who is doing the action?_____
   _____

3. What is the central message of this verse?_____
   _____
   _____

4. Are any promises or blessings given?_____
   _____
   _____

5. Do I reflect the message of this verse?_____
   _____
   _____

Verse Selected_____ Date_____

1. List any action verbs found in this verse._____
   _____

2. What or who is doing the action?_____
   _____

3. What is the central message of this verse?_____
   _____
   _____

4. Are any promises or blessings given?_____
   _____
   _____

5. Do I reflect the message of this verse?_____
   _____
   _____

©1973, John C. Souter. Not to be reproduced.

Verse Glance   5 min.

Verse Selected_____Date_____

1. List any action verbs found in this verse._____
_____

2. What or who is doing the action?_____
_____

3. What is the central message of this verse?_____
_____
_____

4. Are any promises or blessings given?_____
_____
_____

5. Do I reflect the message of this verse?_____
_____
_____

Verse Selected_____Date_____

1. List any action verbs found in this verse._____
_____

2. What or who is doing the action?_____
_____

3. What is the central message of this verse?_____
_____
_____

4. Are any promises or blessings given?_____
_____
_____

5. Do I reflect the message of this verse?_____
_____
_____

©1973, John C. Souter. Not to be reproduced.

Verse Glance   5 min.

Verse Selected_____ Date_____

1. List any action verbs found in this verse._____
   _____

2. What or who is doing the action?_____
   _____

3. What is the central message of this verse?_____
   _____
   _____

4. Are any promises or blessings given?_____
   _____
   _____

5. Do I reflect the message of this verse?_____
   _____
   _____

Verse Selected_____ Date_____

1. List any action verbs found in this verse._____
   _____

2. What or who is doing the action?_____
   _____

3. What is the central message of this verse?_____
   _____
   _____

4. Are any promises or blessings given?_____
   _____
   _____

5. Do I reflect the message of this verse?_____
   _____
   _____

©1973, John C. Souter. Not to be reproduced.

Verse Glance   5 min.

Verse Selected_____ Date_____

1. List any action verbs found in this verse._____
   _____

2. What or who is doing the action?_____
   _____

3. What is the central message of this verse?_____
   _____
   _____

4. Are any promises or blessings given?_____
   _____
   _____

5. Do I reflect the message of this verse?_____
   _____
   _____

Verse Selected_____ Date_____

1. List any action verbs found in this verse._____
   _____

2. What or who is doing the action?_____
   _____

3. What is the central message of this verse?_____
   _____
   _____

4. Are any promises or blessings given?_____
   _____
   _____

5. Do I reflect the message of this verse?_____
   _____
   _____

©1973, John C. Souter. Not to be reproduced.

Verse Glance 5 min.

Verse Selected_____Date_____

1. List any action verbs found in this verse._____
_____

2. What or who is doing the action?_____
_____

3. What is the central message of this verse?_____
_____
_____

4. Are any promises or blessings given?_____
_____
_____

5. Do I reflect the message of this verse?_____
_____
_____

Verse Selected_____Date_____

1. List any action verbs found in this verse._____
_____

2. What or who is doing the action?_____
_____

3. What is the central message of this verse?_____
_____
_____

4. Are any promises or blessings given?_____
_____
_____

5. Do I reflect the message of this verse?_____
_____
_____

© 1973, John C. Souter. Not to be reproduced.

Verse Glance 5 min.

Verse Selected_____ Date_____

1. List any action verbs found in this verse._____
   _____

2. What or who is doing the action?_____
   _____

3. What is the central message of this verse?_____
   _____
   _____

4. Are any promises or blessings given?_____
   _____

5. Do I reflect the message of this verse?_____
   _____
   _____

Verse Selected_____ Date_____

1. List any action verbs found in this verse._____
   _____

2. What or who is doing the action?_____
   _____

3. What is the central message of this verse?_____
   _____
   _____

4. Are any promises or blessings given?_____
   _____

5. Do I reflect the message of this verse?_____
   _____

© 1973, John C. Souter. Not to be reproduced.

Verse Glance   5 min.

Verse Selected_____Date_____

1. List any action verbs found in this verse._____
_____

2. What or who is doing the action?_____
_____

3. What is the central message of this verse?_____
_____
_____

4. Are any promises or blessings given?_____
_____
_____

5. Do I reflect the message of this verse?_____
_____
_____

Verse Selected_____Date_____

1. List any action verbs found in this verse._____
_____

2. What or who is doing the action?_____
_____

3. What is the central message of this verse?_____
_____
_____

4. Are any promises or blessings given?_____
_____
_____

5. Do I reflect the message of this verse?_____
_____
_____

©1973, John C. Souter. Not to be reproduced.

Proverbs Glance — 5 min.

Proverb Selected_____ Date_____

1. What positive qualities are displayed?_____
_____

2. What negative qualities are displayed?_____
_____

3. What basic principle is God teaching in this passage?_____
_____
_____

4. What other Scripture supports this principle?_____
_____

5. How can I benefit from this principle?_____
_____
_____
_____

Proverb Selected_____ Date_____

1. What positive qualities are displayed?_____
_____

2. What negative qualities are displayed?_____
_____

3. What basic principle is God teaching in this passage?_____
_____
_____

4. What other Scripture supports this principle?_____
_____

5. How can I benefit from this principle?_____
_____
_____
_____

©1973, John C. Souter. Not to be reproduced.

Proverbs Glance   5 min.

Proverb Selected_____Date_____

1. What positive qualities are displayed?_____
_____

2. What negative qualities are displayed?_____
_____

3. What basic principle is God teaching in this passage?_____
_____

4. What other Scripture supports this principle?_____
_____

5. How can I benefit from this principle?_____
_____
_____
_____

Proverb Selected_____Date_____

1. What positive qualities are displayed?_____
_____

2. What negative qualities are displayed?_____
_____

3. What basic principle is God teaching in this passage?_____
_____

4. What other Scripture supports this principle?_____
_____

5. How can I benefit from this principle?_____
_____
_____
_____

©1973, John C. Souter. Not to be reproduced.

Proverbs Glance   5 min.

Proverb Selected_____ Date_____

1. What positive qualities are displayed?_____
_____

2. What negative qualities are displayed?_____
_____

3. What basic principle is God teaching in this passage?_____
_____
_____

4. What other Scripture supports this principle?_____
_____

5. How can I benefit from this principle?_____
_____
_____
_____

Proverb Selected_____ Date_____

1. What positive qualities are displayed?_____
_____

2. What negative qualities are displayed?_____
_____

3. What basic principle is God teaching in this passage?_____
_____
_____

4. What other Scripture supports this principle?_____
_____

5. How can I benefit from this principle?_____
_____
_____
_____

© 1973, John C. Souter. Not to be reproduced.

Proverbs Glance — 5 min.

Proverb Selected_____ Date_____

1. What positive qualities are displayed?_____
_____

2. What negative qualities are displayed?_____
_____

3. What basic principle is God teaching in this passage?_____
_____

4. What other Scripture supports this principle?_____
_____

5. How can I benefit from this principle?_____
_____
_____
_____

Proverb Selected_____ Date_____

1. What positive qualities are displayed?_____
_____

2. What negative qualities are displayed?_____
_____

3. What basic principle is God teaching in this passage?_____
_____

4. What other Scripture supports this principle?_____
_____

5. How can I benefit from this principle?_____
_____
_____
_____

©1973, John C. Souter. Not to be reproduced.

Proverbs Glance   5 min.

Proverb Selected_____Date_____

1. What positive qualities are displayed?_____
   _____

2. What negative qualities are displayed?_____
   _____

3. What basic principle is God teaching in this passage?_____
   _____
   _____

4. What other Scripture supports this principle?_____
   _____

5. How can I benefit from this principle?_____
   _____
   _____
   _____

Proverb Selected_____Date_____

1. What positive qualities are displayed?_____
   _____

2. What negative qualities are displayed?_____
   _____

3. What basic principle is God teaching in this passage?_____
   _____
   _____

4. What other Scripture supports this principle?_____
   _____

5. How can I benefit from this principle?_____
   _____
   _____
   _____

Proverbs Glance   5 min.

Proverb Selected_____Date_____

1. What positive qualities are displayed?_____
   _____

2. What negative qualities are displayed?_____
   _____

3. What basic principle is God teaching in this passage?____
   _____
   _____

4. What other Scripture supports this principle?_____
   _____

5. How can I benefit from this principle?_____
   _____
   _____
   _____

Proverb Selected_____Date_____

1. What positive qualities are displayed?_____
   _____

2. What negative qualities are displayed?_____
   _____

3. What basic principle is God teaching in this passage?____
   _____
   _____

4. What other Scripture supports this principle?_____
   _____

5. How can I benefit from this principle?_____
   _____
   _____
   _____

©1973, John C. Souter. Not to be reproduced.

Proverbs Glance 5 min.

Proverb Selected_____ Date_____
1. What positive qualities are displayed?_____
_____

2. What negative qualities are displayed?_____
_____

3. What basic principle is God teaching in this passage?_____
_____
_____

4. What other Scripture supports this principle?_____
_____

5. How can I benefit from this principle?_____
_____
_____
_____

Proverb Selected_____ Date_____
1. What positive qualities are displayed?_____
_____

2. What negative qualities are displayed?_____
_____

3. What basic principle is God teaching in this passage?_____
_____
_____

4. What other Scripture supports this principle?_____
_____

5. How can I benefit from this principle?_____
_____
_____
_____

©1973, John C. Souter. Not to be reproduced.

Proverbs Glance　　5 min.

Proverb Selected_____Date_____
1. What positive qualities are displayed?_____
_____
2. What negative qualities are displayed?_____
_____
3. What basic principle is God teaching in this passage?_____
_____
_____
4. What other Scripture supports this principle?_____
_____
5. How can I benefit from this principle?_____
_____
_____
_____

Proverb Selected_____Date_____
1. What positive qualities are displayed?_____
_____
2. What negative qualities are displayed?_____
_____
3. What basic principle is God teaching in this passage?_____
_____
_____
4. What other Scripture supports this principle?_____
_____
5. How can I benefit from this principle?_____
_____
_____
_____

©1973, John C. Souter. Not to be reproduced.

Proverbs Glance   5 min.

Proverb Selected_____ Date_____

1. What positive qualities are displayed?_____
_____

2. What negative qualities are displayed?_____
_____

3. What basic principle is God teaching in this passage?_____
_____
_____

4. What other Scripture supports this principle?_____
_____

5. How can I benefit from this principle?_____
_____
_____
_____
_____

Proverb Selected_____ Date_____

1. What positive qualities are displayed?_____
_____

2. What negative qualities are displayed?_____
_____

3. What basic principle is God teaching in this passage?_____
_____
_____

4. What other Scripture supports this principle?_____
_____

5. How can I benefit from this principle?_____
_____
_____
_____

©1973, John C. Souter. Not to be reproduced.

Proverbs Glance — 5 min.

Proverb Selected_____ Date_____

1. What positive qualities are displayed?_____
   _____

2. What negative qualities are displayed?_____
   _____

3. What basic principle is God teaching in this passage?____
   _____
   _____

4. What other Scripture supports this principle?_____
   _____

5. How can I benefit from this principle?_____
   _____
   _____
   _____

Proverb Selected_____ Date_____

1. What positive qualities are displayed?_____
   _____

2. What negative qualities are displayed?_____
   _____

3. What basic principle is God teaching in this passage?____
   _____
   _____

4. What other Scripture supports this principle?_____
   _____

5. How can I benefit from this principle?_____
   _____
   _____
   _____

©1973, John C. Souter. Not to be reproduced.

Meditation 5 min.

Passage Selected_____ Date_____

1. Read the passage, considering the meaning of each phrase.
2. Which verse do I want to meditate on today?_____
_____
_____

3. What God gave me from this passage:_____
_____
_____
_____

Passage Selected_____ Date_____

1. Read the passage, considering the meaning of each phrase.
2. Which verse do I want to meditate on today?_____
_____
_____

3. What God gave me from this passage:_____
_____
_____
_____

Passage Selected_____ Date_____

1. Read the passage, considering the meaning of each phrase.
2. Which verse do I want to meditate on today?_____
_____
_____

3. What God gave me from this passage:_____
_____
_____
_____

©1973, John C. Souter. Not to be reproduced.

Meditation 5 min.

Passage Selected _____ Date _____

1. Read the passage, considering the meaning of each phrase.
2. Which verse do I want to meditate on today? _____

_____
_____

3. What God gave me from this passage: _____

_____
_____
_____

Passage Selected _____ Date _____

1. Read the passage, considering the meaning of each phrase.
2. Which verse do I want to meditate on today? _____

_____
_____

3. What God gave me from this passage: _____

_____
_____
_____

Passage Selected _____ Date _____

1. Read the passage, considering the meaning of each phrase.
2. Which verse do I want to meditate on today? _____

_____
_____

3. What God gave me from this passage: _____

_____
_____
_____

© 1973, John C. Souter. Not to be reproduced.

Meditation — 5 min.

Passage Selected _____ Date _____

1. Read the passage, considering the meaning of each phrase.
2. Which verse do I want to meditate on today? _____
   _____
   _____

3. What God gave me from this passage: _____
   _____
   _____
   _____
   _____

Passage Selected _____ Date _____

1. Read the passage, considering the meaning of each phrase.
2. Which verse do I want to meditate on today? _____
   _____
   _____

3. What God gave me from this passage: _____
   _____
   _____
   _____
   _____

Passage Selected _____ Date _____

1. Read the passage, considering the meaning of each phrase.
2. Which verse do I want to meditate on today? _____
   _____
   _____

3. What God gave me from this passage: _____
   _____
   _____
   _____
   _____

© 1973, John C. Souter. Not to be reproduced.

Meditation　　　　5 min.

Passage Selected_____Date_____

1. Read the passage, considering the meaning of each phrase.
2. Which verse do I want to meditate on today?_____
_____
_____

3. What God gave me from this passage:_____
_____
_____
_____

Passage Selected_____Date_____

1. Read the passage, considering the meaning of each phrase.
2. Which verse do I want to meditate on today?_____
_____
_____

3. What God gave me from this passage:_____
_____
_____
_____

Passage Selected_____Date_____

1. Read the passage, considering the meaning of each phrase.
2. Which verse do I want to meditate on today?_____
_____
_____

3. What God gave me from this passage:_____
_____
_____
_____

©1973, John C. Souter. Not to be reproduced.

Meditation   5 min.

Passage Selected_____ Date_____
1. Read the passage, considering the meaning of each phrase.
2. Which verse do I want to meditate on today?_____
_____
_____

3. What God gave me from this passage:_____
_____
_____
_____

Passage Selected_____ Date_____
1. Read the passage, considering the meaning of each phrase.
2. Which verse do I want to meditate on today?_____
_____
_____

3. What God gave me from this passage:_____
_____
_____
_____

Passage Selected_____ Date_____
1. Read the passage, considering the meaning of each phrase.
2. Which verse do I want to meditate on today?_____
_____
_____

3. What God gave me from this passage:_____
_____
_____

©1973, John C. Souter. Not to be reproduced.

Meditation 5 min.

Passage Selected_____ Date_____

1. Read the passage, considering the meaning of each phrase.
2. Which verse do I want to meditate on today?_____
   _____
   _____
3. What God gave me from this passage:_____
   _____
   _____
   _____

Passage Selected_____ Date_____

1. Read the passage, considering the meaning of each phrase.
2. Which verse do I want to meditate on today?_____
   _____
   _____
3. What God gave me from this passage:_____
   _____
   _____
   _____

Passage Selected_____ Date_____

1. Read the passage, considering the meaning of each phrase.
2. Which verse do I want to meditate on today?_____
   _____
   _____
3. What God gave me from this passage:_____
   _____
   _____
   _____

©1973, John C. Souter. Not to be reproduced.

Meditation — 5 min.

Passage Selected_____Date_____
1. Read the passage, considering the meaning of each phrase.
2. Which verse do I want to meditate on today?_____
_____
_____

3. What God gave me from this passage:_____
_____
_____
_____

Passage Selected_____Date_____
1. Read the passage, considering the meaning of each phrase.
2. Which verse do I want to meditate on today?_____
_____
_____

3. What God gave me from this passage:_____
_____
_____
_____

Passage Selected_____Date_____
1. Read the passage, considering the meaning of each phrase.
2. Which verse do I want to meditate on today?_____
_____
_____

3. What God gave me from this passage:_____
_____
_____
_____

©1973, John C. Souter. Not to be reproduced.

Meditation   5 min.

Passage Selected_____Date_____

1. Read the passage, considering the meaning of each phrase.
2. Which verse do I want to meditate on today?_____
   _____
   _____

3. What God gave me from this passage:_____
   _____
   _____
   _____

Passage Selected_____Date_____

1. Read the passage, considering the meaning of each phrase.
2. Which verse do I want to meditate on today?_____
   _____
   _____

3. What God gave me from this passage:_____
   _____
   _____
   _____

Passage Selected_____Date_____

1. Read the passage, considering the meaning of each phrase.
2. Which verse do I want to meditate on today?_____
   _____
   _____

3. What God gave me from this passage:_____
   _____
   _____
   _____

© 1973, John C. Souter. Not to be reproduced.

Meditation   5 min.

Passage Selected _____ Date _____

1. Read the passage, considering the meaning of each phrase.
2. Which verse do I want to meditate on today? _____
_____
_____
3. What God gave me from this passage: _____
_____
_____
_____
_____

Passage Selected _____ Date _____

1. Read the passage, considering the meaning of each phrase.
2. Which verse do I want to meditate on today? _____
_____
_____
3. What God gave me from this passage: _____
_____
_____
_____
_____

Passage Selected _____ Date _____

1. Read the passage, considering the meaning of each phrase.
2. Which verse do I want to meditate on today? _____
_____
_____
3. What God gave me from this passage: _____
_____
_____
_____
_____

© 1973, John C. Souter. Not to be reproduced.

Meditation 5 min.

Passage Selected_____Date_____
1. Read the passage, considering the meaning of each phrase.
2. Which verse do I want to meditate on today?_____
_____
_____
3. What God gave me from this passage:_____
_____
_____
_____

Passage Selected_____Date_____
1. Read the passage, considering the meaning of each phrase.
2. Which verse do I want to meditate on today?_____
_____
_____
3. What God gave me from this passage:_____
_____
_____
_____

Passage Selected_____Date_____
1. Read the passage, considering the meaning of each phrase.
2. Which verse do I want to meditate on today?_____
_____
_____
3. What God gave me from this passage:_____
_____
_____
_____

©1973, John C. Souter. Not to be reproduced.

Psalm Glance　　　　5 min.

Psalm Selected_____ Date_____

1. Check the type of Psalm:
   - ☐ Messianic or Prophetic　　☐ Nature
   - ☐ Instructional　　　　　　 ☐ Praise
   - ☐ Historical　　　　　　　　☐ Prayer

2. What is this Psalm about?_____
   _____
   _____

3. Are any blessings promised?_____
   _____
   _____

4. What does this Psalm say to me?_____
   _____
   _____

Psalm Selected_____ Date_____

1. Check the type of Psalm:
   - ☐ Messianic or Prophetic　　☐ Nature
   - ☐ Instructional　　　　　　 ☐ Praise
   - ☐ Historical　　　　　　　　☐ Prayer

2. What is this Psalm about?_____
   _____
   _____

3. Are any blessings promised?_____
   _____
   _____

4. What does this Psalm say to me?_____
   _____
   _____

©1973, John C. Souter. Not to be reproduced.

Psalm Glance   5 min.

Psalm Selected_____Date_____

1. Check the type of Psalm:
   - ☐ Messianic or Prophetic   ☐ Nature
   - ☐ Instructional   ☐ Praise
   - ☐ Historical   ☐ Prayer
2. What is this Psalm about?_____
   _____
   _____
3. Are any blessings promised?_____
   _____
   _____
4. What does this Psalm say to me?_____
   _____
   _____

Psalm Selected_____Date_____

1. Check the type of Psalm:
   - ☐ Messianic or Prophetic   ☐ Nature
   - ☐ Instructional   ☐ Praise
   - ☐ Historical   ☐ Prayer
2. What is this Psalm about?_____
   _____
   _____
3. Are any blessings promised?_____
   _____
   _____
4. What does this Psalm say to me?_____
   _____
   _____

©1973, John C. Souter. Not to be reproduced.

Psalm Glance 5 min.

Psalm Selected_____ Date_____

1. Check the type of Psalm:
   - ☐ Messianic or Prophetic
   - ☐ Instructional
   - ☐ Historical
   - ☐ Nature
   - ☐ Praise
   - ☐ Prayer

2. What is this Psalm about?_____
   _____
   _____

3. Are any blessings promised?_____
   _____
   _____

4. What does this Psalm say to me?_____
   _____
   _____

Psalm Selected_____ Date_____

1. Check the type of Psalm:
   - ☐ Messianic or Prophetic
   - ☐ Instructional
   - ☐ Historical
   - ☐ Nature
   - ☐ Praise
   - ☐ Prayer

2. What is this Psalm about?_____
   _____
   _____

3. Are any blessings promised?_____
   _____
   _____

4. What does this Psalm say to me?_____
   _____

© 1973, John C. Souter. Not to be reproduced.

Psalm Glance   5 min.

Psalm Selected_____ Date_____

1. Check the type of Psalm:
   - ☐ Messianic or Prophetic   ☐ Nature
   - ☐ Instructional   ☐ Praise
   - ☐ Historical   ☐ Prayer

2. What is this Psalm about?_____
   _____
   _____

3. Are any blessings promised?_____
   _____
   _____

4. What does this Psalm say to me?_____
   _____
   _____

Psalm Selected_____ Date_____

1. Check the type of Psalm:
   - ☐ Messianic or Prophetic   ☐ Nature
   - ☐ Instructional   ☐ Praise
   - ☐ Historical   ☐ Prayer

2. What is this Psalm about?_____
   _____
   _____

3. Are any blessings promised?_____
   _____
   _____

4. What does this Psalm say to me?_____
   _____
   _____

©1973, John C. Souter. Not to be reproduced.

Psalm Glance　　　　*5 min.*

Psalm Selected_____ Date_____

1. Check the type of Psalm:
   - ☐ Messianic or Prophetic　　☐ Nature
   - ☐ Instructional　　　　　　 ☐ Praise
   - ☐ Historical　　　　　　　 ☐ Prayer
2. What is this Psalm about?_____
   _____
   _____
3. Are any blessings promised?_____
   _____
   _____
4. What does this Psalm say to me?_____
   _____
   _____

Psalm Selected_____ Date_____

1. Check the type of Psalm:
   - ☐ Messianic or Prophetic　　☐ Nature
   - ☐ Instructional　　　　　　 ☐ Praise
   - ☐ Historical　　　　　　　 ☐ Prayer
2. What is this Psalm about?_____
   _____
   _____
3. Are any blessings promised?_____
   _____
   _____
4. What does this Psalm say to me?_____
   _____
   _____

© 1973, John C. Souter. Not to be reproduced.

Psalm Glance   5 min.

Psalm Selected_____ Date_____

1. Check the type of Psalm:
   - ☐ Messianic or Prophetic   ☐ Nature
   - ☐ Instructional   ☐ Praise
   - ☐ Historical   ☐ Prayer

2. What is this Psalm about?_____
   _____
   _____

3. Are any blessings promised?_____
   _____
   _____

4. What does this Psalm say to me?_____
   _____
   _____

Psalm Selected_____ Date_____

1. Check the type of Psalm:
   - ☐ Messianic or Prophetic   ☐ Nature
   - ☐ Instructional   ☐ Praise
   - ☐ Historical   ☐ Prayer

2. What is this Psalm about?_____
   _____
   _____

3. Are any blessings promised?_____
   _____
   _____

4. What does this Psalm say to me?_____
   _____
   _____

Psalm Glance 5 min.

Psalm Selected_____ Date_____

1. Check the type of Psalm:
   - ☐ Messianic or Prophetic
   - ☐ Instructional
   - ☐ Historical
   - ☐ Nature
   - ☐ Praise
   - ☐ Prayer
2. What is this Psalm about?_____
   _____
   _____
3. Are any blessings promised?_____
   _____
   _____
4. What does this Psalm say to me?_____
   _____
   _____

Psalm Selected_____ Date_____

1. Check the type of Psalm:
   - ☐ Messianic or Prophetic
   - ☐ Instructional
   - ☐ Historical
   - ☐ Nature
   - ☐ Praise
   - ☐ Prayer
2. What is this Psalm about?_____
   _____
   _____
3. Are any blessings promised?_____
   _____
   _____
4. What does this Psalm say to me?_____
   _____
   _____

©1973, John C. Souter. Not to be reproduced.

Psalm Glance　　　　5 min.

Psalm Selected_____Date_____

1. Check the type of Psalm:
   - ☐ Messianic or Prophetic
   - ☐ Instructional
   - ☐ Historical
   - ☐ Nature
   - ☐ Praise
   - ☐ Prayer

2. What is this Psalm about?_____
   _____
   _____

3. Are any blessings promised?_____
   _____
   _____

4. What does this Psalm say to me?_____
   _____
   _____

Psalm Selected_____Date_____

1. Check the type of Psalm:
   - ☐ Messianic or Prophetic
   - ☐ Instructional
   - ☐ Historical
   - ☐ Nature
   - ☐ Praise
   - ☐ Prayer

2. What is this Psalm about?_____
   _____
   _____

3. Are any blessings promised?_____
   _____
   _____

4. What does this Psalm say to me?_____
   _____
   _____

©1973, John C. Souter. Not to be reproduced.

Psalm Glance　　　　　5 min.

Psalm Selected_____ Date_____

1. Check the type of Psalm:
   - ☐ Messianic or Prophetic　　☐ Nature
   - ☐ Instructional　　　　　　　☐ Praise
   - ☐ Historical　　　　　　　　☐ Prayer

2. What is this Psalm about?_____
   _____
   _____

3. Are any blessings promised?_____
   _____
   _____

4. What does this Psalm say to me?_____
   _____
   _____

Psalm Selected_____ Date_____

1. Check the type of Psalm:
   - ☐ Messianic or Prophetic　　☐ Nature
   - ☐ Instructional　　　　　　　☐ Praise
   - ☐ Historical　　　　　　　　☐ Prayer

2. What is this Psalm about?_____
   _____
   _____

3. Are any blessings promised?_____
   _____
   _____

4. What does this Psalm say to me?_____
   _____
   _____

©1973, John C. Souter. Not to be reproduced.

Psalm Glance   5 min.

Psalm Selected_____Date_____

1. Check the type of Psalm:
   - ☐ Messianic or Prophetic   ☐ Nature
   - ☐ Instructional   ☐ Praise
   - ☐ Historical   ☐ Prayer
2. What is this Psalm about?_____
   _____
   _____
3. Are any blessings promised?_____
   _____
   _____
4. What does this Psalm say to me?_____
   _____
   _____

Psalm Selected_____Date_____

1. Check the type of Psalm:
   - ☐ Messianic or Prophetic   ☐ Nature
   - ☐ Instructional   ☐ Praise
   - ☐ Historical   ☐ Prayer
2. What is this Psalm about?_____
   _____
   _____
3. Are any blessings promised?_____
   _____
   _____
4. What does this Psalm say to me?_____
   _____
   _____

©1973, John C. Souter. Not to be reproduced.

Paragraph Glance   5 min.

Book_____ No. of Chapters_____

Write the paragraph references on the left. Summarize the contents of each paragraph on the right. Date each entry.

REFERENCE	SUMMARY	DATE

Paragraph Glance 5 min.

Book_____No. of Chapters_____

Write the paragraph references on the left. Summarize the contents of each paragraph on the right. Date each entry.

REFERENCE	SUMMARY	DATE

Paragraph Glance — 5 min.

Book _____ No. of Chapters _____

Write the paragraph references on the left. Summarize the contents of each paragraph on the right. Date each entry.

REFERENCE	SUMMARY	DATE

Paragraph Glance   5 min.

Book_____No. of Chapters_____

Write the paragraph references on the left. Summarize the contents of each paragraph on the right. Date each entry.

REFERENCE	SUMMARY	DATE

© 1973, John C. Souter. Not to be reproduced.

Paragraph Glance — 5 min.

Book _____ No. of Chapters _____

Write the paragraph references on the left. Summarize the contents of each paragraph on the right. Date each entry.

REFERENCE	SUMMARY	DATE

©1973, John C. Souter. Not to be reproduced.

Paragraph Glance   5 min.

Book_____ No. of Chapters_____

Write the paragraph references on the left. Summarize the contents of each paragraph on the right. Date each entry.

REFERENCE	SUMMARY	DATE

© 1973, John C. Souter. Not to be reproduced.

Paragraph Glance   5 min.

Book_____No. of Chapters_____

Write the paragraph references on the left. Summarize the contents of each paragraph on the right. Date each entry.

REFERENCE	SUMMARY	DATE

Paragraph Glance   5 min.

Book_____No. of Chapters_____

Write the paragraph references on the left. Summarize the contents of each paragraph on the right. Date each entry.

REFERENCE	SUMMARY	DATE

Paragraph Glance   5 min.

Book_____No. of Chapters_____

Write the paragraph references on the left. Summarize the contents of each paragraph on the right. Date each entry.

REFERENCE	SUMMARY	DATE

Paragraph Glance   5 min.

Book_____ No. of Chapters_____

Write the paragraph references on the left. Summarize the contents of each paragraph on the right. Date each entry.

REFERENCE	SUMMARY	DATE

Paragraph Glance 5 min.

Book_____ No. of Chapters_____

Write the paragraph references on the left. Summarize the contents of each paragraph on the right. Date each entry.

REFERENCE	SUMMARY	DATE

Paragraph Glance   5 min.

Book_____ No. of Chapters_____

Write the paragraph references on the left. Summarize the contents of each paragraph on the right. Date each entry.

REFERENCE	SUMMARY	DATE

Paragraph Glance — 5 min.

Book_____No. of Chapters_____

Write the paragraph references on the left. Summarize the contents of each paragraph on the right. Date each entry.

REFERENCE	SUMMARY	DATE

© 1973, John C. Souter. Not to be reproduced.

Paragraph Glance   5 min.

Book_____ No. of Chapters_____

Write the paragraph references on the left. Summarize the contents of each paragraph on the right. Date each entry.

REFERENCE	SUMMARY	DATE

Paragraph Glance   5 min.

Book_____ No. of Chapters_____

Write the paragraph references on the left. Summarize the contents of each paragraph on the right. Date each entry.

REFERENCE	SUMMARY	DATE

Paragraph Glance　　5 min.

Book_____No. of Chapters_____

Write the paragraph references on the left. Summarize the contents of each paragraph on the right. Date each entry.

REFERENCE	SUMMARY	DATE

Paragraph Glance 5 min.

Book_____ No. of Chapters_____

Write the paragraph references on the left. Summarize the contents of each paragraph on the right. Date each entry.

REFERENCE	SUMMARY	DATE

© 1973, John C. Souter. Not to be reproduced.

Paragraph Glance 5 min.

Book_____No. of Chapters_____

Write the paragraph references on the left. Summarize the contents of each paragraph on the right. Date each entry.

REFERENCE	SUMMARY	DATE

© 1973, John C. Souter. Not to be reproduced.

Paragraph Glance　　5 min.

Book_____No. of Chapters_____

Write the paragraph references on the left. Summarize the contents of each paragraph on the right. Date each entry.

REFERENCE	SUMMARY	DATE

© 1973, John C. Souter. Not to be reproduced.

Paragraph Glance 5 min.

Book_____ No. of Chapters_____

Write the paragraph references on the left. Summarize the contents of each paragraph on the right. Date each entry.

REFERENCE	SUMMARY	DATE

© 1973, John C. Souter. Not to be reproduced.

Prophecy Glance 5 min.

Book Selected_____

1. Write the passage references on the left.
2. Summarize the contents of each paragraph. If it contains a prophecy write "P" at the right.
3. Spend no more than 5 minutes per passage.

REFERENCE	SUMMARY	DATE

Prophecy Glance — 5 min.

Book Selected _____

1. Write the passage references on the left.
2. Summarize the contents of each paragraph. If it contains a prophecy write "P" at the right.
3. Spend no more than 5 minutes per passage.

REFERENCE	SUMMARY	DATE

©1973, John C. Souter. Not to be reproduced.

Prophecy Glance   5 min.

Book Selected _____

1. Write the passage references on the left.
2. Summarize the contents of each paragraph. If it contains a prophecy write "P" at the right.
3. Spend no more than 5 minutes per passage.

REFERENCE	SUMMARY	DATE

© 1973, John C. Souter. Not to be reproduced.

Prophecy Glance — 5 min.

Book Selected_____

1. Write the passage references on the left.
2. Summarize the contents of each paragraph. If it contains a prophecy write "P" at the right.
3. Spend no more than 5 minutes per passage.

REFERENCE	SUMMARY	DATE

Prophecy Glance — 5 min.

Book Selected _____

1. Write the passage references on the left.
2. Summarize the contents of each paragraph. If it contains a prophecy write "P" at the right.
3. Spend no more than 5 minutes per passage.

REFERENCE	SUMMARY	DATE

© 1973, John C. Souter. Not to be reproduced.

Prophecy Glance   5 min.

Book Selected_____

1. Write the passage references on the left.
2. Summarize the contents of each paragraph. If it contains a prophecy write "P" at the right.
3. Spend no more than 5 minutes per passage.

REFERENCE   SUMMARY   DATE

Prophecy Glance — 5 min.

Book Selected _____

1. Write the passage references on the left.
2. Summarize the contents of each paragraph. If it contains a prophecy write "P" at the right.
3. Spend no more than 5 minutes per passage.

REFERENCE	SUMMARY	DATE

Prophecy Glance   5 min.

Book Selected_____

1. Write the passage references on the left.
2. Summarize the contents of each paragraph. If it contains a prophecy write "P" at the right.
3. Spend no more than 5 minutes per passage.

REFERENCE	SUMMARY	DATE

Prophecy Glance — 5 min.

Book Selected_____

1. Write the passage references on the left.
2. Summarize the contents of each paragraph. If it contains a prophecy write "P" at the right.
3. Spend no more than 5 minutes per passage.

REFERENCE	SUMMARY	DATE

Prophecy Glance 5 min.

Book Selected_____

1. Write the passage references on the left.
2. Summarize the contents of each paragraph. If it contains a prophecy write "P" at the right.
3. Spend no more than 5 minutes per passage.

REFERENCE   SUMMARY   DATE

© 1973, John C. Souter. Not to be reproduced.

Prophecy Glance   5 min.

Book Selected _____

1. Write the passage references on the left.
2. Summarize the contents of each paragraph. If it contains a prophecy write "P" at the right.
3. Spend no more than 5 minutes per passage.

REFERENCE	SUMMARY	DATE

Prophecy Glance   5 min.

Book Selected_____

1. Write the passage references on the left.
2. Summarize the contents of each paragraph. If it contains a prophecy write "P" at the right.
3. Spend no more than 5 minutes per passage.

REFERENCE	SUMMARY	DATE

©1973, John C. Souter. Not to be reproduced.

Prophecy Glance   5 min.

Book Selected_____

1. Write the passage references on the left.
2. Summarize the contents of each paragraph. If it contains a prophecy write "P" at the right.
3. Spend no more than 5 minutes per passage.

REFERENCE　　　　　　SUMMARY　　　　　　　　DATE

Prophecy Glance   5 min.

Book Selected_____

1. Write the passage references on the left.
2. Summarize the contents of each paragraph. If it contains a prophecy write "P" at the right.
3. Spend no more than 5 minutes per passage.

REFERENCE   SUMMARY   DATE

Prophecy Glance — 5 min.

Book Selected _____

1. Write the passage references on the left.
2. Summarize the contents of each paragraph. If it contains a prophecy write "P" at the right.
3. Spend no more than 5 minutes per passage.

REFERENCE	SUMMARY	DATE

Prophecy Glance — 5 min.

Book Selected _____

1. Write the passage references on the left.
2. Summarize the contents of each paragraph. If it contains a prophecy write "P" at the right.
3. Spend no more than 5 minutes per passage.

REFERENCE	SUMMARY	DATE

Prophecy Glance　　　5 min.

Book Selected _____

1. Write the passage references on the left.
2. Summarize the contents of each paragraph. If it contains a prophecy write "P" at the right.
3. Spend no more than 5 minutes per passage.

REFERENCE　　　　　SUMMARY　　　　　DATE

©1973, John C. Souter. Not to be reproduced.

Prophecy Glance — 5 min.

Book Selected _____

1. Write the passage references on the left.
2. Summarize the contents of each paragraph. If it contains a prophecy write "P" at the right.
3. Spend no more than 5 minutes per passage.

REFERENCE	SUMMARY	DATE

© 1973, John C. Souter. Not to be reproduced.

Prophecy Glance — 5 min.

Book Selected_____

1. Write the passage references on the left.
2. Summarize the contents of each paragraph. If it contains a prophecy write "P" at the right.
3. Spend no more than 5 minutes per passage.

REFERENCE	SUMMARY	DATE

Prophecy Glance — 5 min.

Book Selected _____

1. Write the passage references on the left.
2. Summarize the contents of each paragraph. If it contains a prophecy write "P" at the right.
3. Spend no more than 5 minutes per passage.

REFERENCE	SUMMARY	DATE

Paraphrase 5 min.

Verses Selected_____ Date_____

1. I am using the following two translations:_____
   _____

2. Here is my paraphrase of the passage:_____
   _____
   _____
   _____
   _____
   _____
   _____
   _____
   _____
   _____
   _____

Verses Selected_____ Date_____

1. I am using the following two translations:_____
   _____

2. Here is my paraphrase of the passage:_____
   _____
   _____
   _____
   _____
   _____
   _____
   _____
   _____
   _____
   _____

© 1973, John C. Souter. Not to be reproduced.

Paraphrase — 5 min.

Verses Selected_____Date_____

1. I am using the following two translations:_____

_____

2. Here is my paraphrase of the passage:_____

_____
_____
_____
_____
_____
_____
_____
_____
_____
_____

Verses Selected_____Date_____

1. I am using the following two translations:_____

_____

2. Here is my paraphrase of the passage:_____

_____
_____
_____
_____
_____
_____
_____
_____
_____
_____

Paraphrase 5 min.

Verses Selected_____ Date_____

1. I am using the following two translations:_____

_____

2. Here is my paraphrase of the passage:_____

_____

_____

_____

_____

_____

_____

_____

_____

_____

_____

_____

Verses Selected_____ Date_____

1. I am using the following two translations:_____

_____

2. Here is my paraphrase of the passage:_____

_____

_____

_____

_____

_____

_____

_____

_____

_____

_____

_____

© 1973, John C. Souter. Not to be reproduced.

Paraphrase — 5 min.

Verses Selected_____Date_____

1. I am using the following two translations:_____
_____

2. Here is my paraphrase of the passage:_____
_____
_____
_____
_____
_____
_____
_____
_____
_____
_____

Verses Selected_____Date_____

1. I am using the following two translations:_____
_____

2. Here is my paraphrase of the passage:_____
_____
_____
_____
_____
_____
_____
_____
_____
_____
_____

©1973, John C. Souter. Not to be reproduced.

Paraphrase   5 min.

Verses Selected_____ Date_____

1. I am using the following two translations:_____

_____

2. Here is my paraphrase of the passage:_____

_____
_____
_____
_____
_____
_____
_____
_____
_____
_____
_____

Verses Selected_____ Date_____

1. I am using the following two translations:_____

_____

2. Here is my paraphrase of the passage:_____

_____
_____
_____
_____
_____
_____
_____
_____
_____
_____
_____

©1973, John C. Souter. Not to be reproduced.

Paraphrase 5 min.

Verses Selected_____ Date_____

1. I am using the following two translations:_____
_____

2. Here is my paraphrase of the passage:_____
_____
_____
_____
_____
_____
_____
_____
_____
_____
_____

Verses Selected_____ Date_____

1. I am using the following two translations:_____
_____

2. Here is my paraphrase of the passage:_____
_____
_____
_____
_____
_____
_____
_____
_____
_____
_____

© 1973, John C. Souter. Not to be reproduced.

Paraphrase — 5 min.

Verses Selected _____ Date _____

1. I am using the following two translations: _____
_____

2. Here is my paraphrase of the passage: _____
_____
_____
_____
_____
_____
_____
_____
_____
_____
_____
_____

Verses Selected _____ Date _____

1. I am using the following two translations: _____
_____

2. Here is my paraphrase of the passage: _____
_____
_____
_____
_____
_____
_____
_____
_____
_____
_____
_____

©1973, John C. Souter. Not to be reproduced.

Paraphrase — *5 min.*

Verses Selected_____Date_____

1. I am using the following two translations:_____

_____

2. Here is my paraphrase of the passage:_____

_____
_____
_____
_____
_____
_____
_____
_____
_____

Verses Selected_____Date_____

1. I am using the following two translations:_____

_____

2. Here is my paraphrase of the passage:_____

_____
_____
_____
_____
_____
_____
_____
_____
_____

©1973, John C. Souter. Not to be reproduced.

Paraphrase   5 min.

Verses Selected_____ Date_____

1. I am using the following two translations:_____

2. Here is my paraphrase of the passage:_____

_____
_____
_____
_____
_____
_____
_____
_____
_____
_____
_____
_____

Verses Selected_____ Date_____

1. I am using the following two translations:_____

2. Here is my paraphrase of the passage:_____

_____
_____
_____
_____
_____
_____
_____
_____
_____
_____
_____
_____

© 1973, John C. Souter. Not to be reproduced.

Paraphrase 5 min.

Verses Selected_____ Date_____

1. I am using the following two translations:_____
_____

2. Here is my paraphrase of the passage:_____
_____
_____
_____
_____
_____
_____
_____
_____
_____
_____
_____

Verses Selected_____ Date_____

1. I am using the following two translations:_____
_____

2. Here is my paraphrase of the passage:_____
_____
_____
_____
_____
_____
_____
_____
_____
_____
_____
_____

©1973, John C. Souter. Not to be reproduced.

Law Study — 15 min.

Passage Selected __Roman 12:1__ Date __2/13/77__

1. What does the passage command to be done or not to be done?
   Give ourselves as a living sacrifice Holy & Unblemished and acceptable in Gods sight which is our form of worship.

2. Was this law aimed at a certain group (age, occupation, etc.)?
   believers

3. Would their need apply to me? I hope so (I know (John))

4. Has this law been done away with in some other part of scripture?
   No it is applicable to all believers past, present, & future

5. What is God's unchangeable principle behind this law? In offering our bodies as a living sacrifice we must be HOLY AND be ACCEPTABLE in Gods sight. Then offering all our time, talents, money, possessions etc., for God to use. Present means totally giving & not taking back.

6. Are there any passages in the New Testament which teach this principle? (Use cross-references) 1 Peter 2:5, Romans 6:13 Heb 13:16

7. What has God taught me for practical living from this passage?
   Easy Me - Music (when I stopped getting into worldly music)
   Geoff - Drugs
   Struggle Me - Farm shop
   Geoff - Job

©1973, John C. Souter. Not to be reproduced.   119

Give it all to God & you won't hassle with it later

Law Study — 15 min.

Passage Selected __Heb. 13:15__ Date __2/16/77__

1. What does the passage command to be done or not to be done?
   Offer up spiritual sacrifices to God through Jesus (Mediator between God + Man)

2. Was this law aimed at a certain group (age, occupation, etc.)?
   all born again believers

3. Would their need apply to me? Definitly

4. Has this law been done away with in some other part of scripture?
   No

5. What is God's unchangeable principle behind this law? that (1 Peter 1:3 Phil 4:4-6) regardless of the circumstances were are to offer sacrifices of praise we were created for praise (Isaih 43:21)

6. Are there any passages in the New Testament which teach this principle? (Use cross-references) (1 Thess 5:18) thanks in all circumstances (Eph 5:20)(ps.150:6) everything is to praise God. (ps 43:3-5) God will Help us

7. What has God taught me for practical living from this passage?
   Especially in Trials, bummers, etc. we must praise God. There is power in this praise & God honors it.

©1973, John C. Souter. Not to be reproduced.

Law Study — 15 min.

Passage Selected **Phil 2:4** Date **2/25/77**

1. What does the passage command to be done or not to be done?
   With unselfishness look to others needs intrests first

2. Was this law aimed at a certain group (age, occupation, etc.)?
   NO

3. Would their need apply to me? yes

4. Has this law been done away with in some other part of scripture?
   NO

5. What is God's unchangeable principle behind this law? Jesus comanded us to serve others. To count others (Luke 22:26) Phil 2:3 Better than ourselves. To be humble. washing others feet

6. Are there any passages in the New Testament which teach this principle? (Use cross-references) Luke 22:26, Phil Rom 15:1-3 bear one anothers burdens

7. What has God taught me for practical living from this passage? to sacrifies myself for others benifit ex. Renny, Pastor Harbaugh etc.

©1973, John C. Souter. Not to be reproduced.

Law Study　　　　　　　　15 min.

Passage Selected_____Date_____

1. What does the passage command to be done or not to be done?____
   _____
   _____
   _____

2. Was this law aimed at a certain group (age, occupation, etc.)?_____
   _____

3. Would their need apply to me?_____
4. Has this law been done away with in some other part of scripture?
   _____
   _____
   _____

5. What is God's unchangeable principle behind this law?_____
   _____
   _____
   _____
   _____
   _____

6. Are there any passages in the New Testament which teach this principle? (Use cross-references)_____
   _____
   _____
   _____
   _____

7. What has God taught me for practical living from this passage?____
   _____
   _____
   _____
   _____

©1973, John C. Souter. Not to be reproduced.

Law Study — 15 min.

Passage Selected_____ Date_____

1. What does the passage command to be done or not to be done?____
_____
_____
_____

2. Was this law aimed at a certain group (age, occupation, etc.)?_____
_____

3. Would their need apply to me?_____

4. Has this law been done away with in some other part of scripture?
_____
_____
_____

5. What is God's unchangeable principle behind this law?_____
_____
_____
_____
_____

6. Are there any passages in the New Testament which teach this principle? (Use cross-references)_____
_____
_____
_____
_____

7. What has God taught me for practical living from this passage?____
_____
_____
_____
_____

© 1973, John C. Souter. Not to be reproduced.

Law Study　　　　　　　　　　　15 min.

Passage Selected_____Date_____

1. What does the passage command to be done or not to be done?____
   _____
   _____
   _____

2. Was this law aimed at a certain group (age, occupation, etc.)?_____
   _____

3. Would their need apply to me?_____

4. Has this law been done away with in some other part of scripture?
   _____
   _____
   _____

5. What is God's unchangeable principle behind this law?_____
   _____
   _____
   _____
   _____

6. Are there any passages in the New Testament which teach this principle? (Use cross-references)_____
   _____
   _____
   _____

7. What has God taught me for practical living from this passage?____
   _____
   _____
   _____
   _____

©1973, John C. Souter. Not to be reproduced.

Law Study *15 min.*

Passage Selected_____Date_____

1. What does the passage command to be done or not to be done?____
   _____
   _____

2. Was this law aimed at a certain group (age, occupation, etc.)?_____
   _____

3. Would their need apply to me?_____

4. Has this law been done away with in some other part of scripture?
   _____
   _____

5. What is God's unchangeable principle behind this law?_____
   _____
   _____
   _____
   _____

6. Are there any passages in the New Testament which teach this principle? (Use cross-references)_____
   _____
   _____
   _____

7. What has God taught me for practical living from this passage?_____
   _____
   _____
   _____

©1973, John C. Souter. Not to be reproduced.

Law Study   15 min.

Passage Selected_____Date_____

1. What does the passage command to be done or not to be done?_____
   _____
   _____

2. Was this law aimed at a certain group (age, occupation, etc.)?_____
   _____

3. Would their need apply to me?_____
4. Has this law been done away with in some other part of scripture?
   _____
   _____
   _____

5. What is God's unchangeable principle behind this law?_____
   _____
   _____
   _____
   _____

6. Are there any passages in the New Testament which teach this principle? (Use cross-references)_____
   _____
   _____
   _____

7. What has God taught me for practical living from this passage?_____
   _____
   _____
   _____

©1973, John C. Souter. Not to be reproduced.

Law Study 15 min.

Passage Selected_____Date_____

1. What does the passage command to be done or not to be done?____
   _____
   _____
   _____

2. Was this law aimed at a certain group (age, occupation, etc.)?_____

3. Would their need apply to me?_____

4. Has this law been done away with in some other part of scripture?
   _____
   _____
   _____

5. What is God's unchangeable principle behind this law?_____
   _____
   _____
   _____
   _____

6. Are there any passages in the New Testament which teach this principle? (Use cross-references)_____
   _____
   _____
   _____

7. What has God taught me for practical living from this passage?____
   _____
   _____
   _____

©1973, John C. Souter. Not to be reproduced.

Law Study — 15 min.

Passage Selected_____ Date_____

1. What does the passage command to be done or not to be done?_____

2. Was this law aimed at a certain group (age, occupation, etc.)?_____

3. Would their need apply to me?_____

4. Has this law been done away with in some other part of scripture?

5. What is God's unchangeable principle behind this law?_____

6. Are there any passages in the New Testament which teach this principle? (Use cross-references)_____

7. What has God taught me for practical living from this passage?_____

©1973, John C. Souter. Not to be reproduced.

Prophecy Study 15 min.

Passage Selected_____ Date_____

1. Which prophet is speaking?_____
2. Who is he speaking to?_____
3. Why was the prophecy given?_____

4. How did the people of that day respond?_____

5. What immediate event does the prophecy foretell?_____

6. Is there a second (long range) prophecy given?_____

7. Explain how each prophecy has been fulfilled. (Give fulfillment references if possible)._____
   a._____

   b._____

8. What basic principle was God teaching?_____

©1973, John C. Souter. Not to be reproduced.

Prophecy Study   15 min.

Passage Selected_____ Date_____

1. Which prophet is speaking?_____
2. Who is he speaking to?_____
3. Why was the prophecy given?_____
_____

4. How did the people of that day respond?_____
_____

5. What immediate event does the prophecy foretell?___
_____
_____

6. Is there a second (long range) prophecy given?_____
_____
_____

7. Explain how each prophecy has been fulfilled. (Give fulfillment references if possible)._____
    a._____
_____

    b._____
_____

8. What basic principle was God teaching?_____
_____
_____

©1973, John C. Souter. Not to be reproduced.

Prophecy Study   15 min.

Passage Selected_____ Date_____

1. Which prophet is speaking?_____
2. Who is he speaking to?_____
3. Why was the prophecy given?_____
   _____

4. How did the people of that day respond?_____
   _____

5. What immediate event does the prophecy foretell?____
   _____
   _____

6. Is there a second (long range) prophecy given?____
   _____
   _____

7. Explain how each prophecy has been fulfilled. (Give fulfillment references if possible)._____

   a._____
   _____
   _____

   b._____
   _____
   _____

8. What basic principle was God teaching?_____
   _____
   _____

©1973, John C. Souter. Not to be reproduced.

Prophecy Study 15 min.

Passage Selected_____ Date_____

1. Which prophet is speaking?_____
2. Who is he speaking to?_____
3. Why was the prophecy given?_____
_____
_____

4. How did the people of that day respond?_____
_____
_____

5. What immediate event does the prophecy foretell?_____
_____
_____
_____

6. Is there a second (long range) prophecy given?_____
_____
_____
_____

7. Explain how each prophecy has been fulfilled. (Give fulfillment references if possible)._____
    a._____
_____
_____

    b._____
_____
_____

8. What basic principle was God teaching?_____
_____
_____

© 1973, John C. Souter. Not to be reproduced.

Prophecy Study   15 min.

Passage Selected_____Date_____

1. Which prophet is speaking?_____
2. Who is he speaking to?_____
3. Why was the prophecy given?_____
_____
_____

4. How did the people of that day respond?_____
_____
_____

5. What immediate event does the prophecy foretell?_____
_____
_____
_____

6. Is there a second (long range) prophecy given?_____
_____
_____
_____

7. Explain how each prophecy has been fulfilled. (Give fulfillment references if possible)._____
    a._____
_____
_____
    b._____
_____
_____

8. What basic principle was God teaching?_____
_____
_____
_____

©1973, John C. Souter. Not to be reproduced.

Prophecy Study — 15 min.

Passage Selected _____ Date _____

1. Which prophet is speaking? _____
2. Who is he speaking to? _____
3. Why was the prophecy given? _____
_____
_____

4. How did the people of that day respond? _____
_____
_____

5. What immediate event does the prophecy foretell? _____
_____
_____
_____

6. Is there a second (long range) prophecy given? _____
_____
_____
_____

7. Explain how each prophecy has been fulfilled. (Give fulfillment references if possible). _____
    a. _____
_____
_____

    b. _____
_____
_____

8. What basic principle was God teaching? _____
_____
_____

©1973, John C. Souter. Not to be reproduced.

Prophecy Study   15 min.

Passage Selected_____ Date_____

1. Which prophet is speaking?_____
2. Who is he speaking to?_____
3. Why was the prophecy given?_____
   _____
   _____

4. How did the people of that day respond?_____
   _____
   _____

5. What immediate event does the prophecy foretell?___
   _____
   _____
   _____

6. Is there a second (long range) prophecy given?_____
   _____
   _____
   _____

7. Explain how each prophecy has been fulfilled. (Give fulfillment references if possible)._____
   a._____
   _____
   _____
   b._____
   _____
   _____

8. What basic principle was God teaching?_____
   _____
   _____
   _____

©1973, John C. Souter. Not to be reproduced.

Prophecy Study — 15 min.

Passage Selected_____ Date_____

1. Which prophet is speaking?_____
2. Who is he speaking to?_____
3. Why was the prophecy given?_____

4. How did the people of that day respond?_____

5. What immediate event does the prophecy foretell?_____

6. Is there a second (long range) prophecy given?_____

7. Explain how each prophecy has been fulfilled. (Give fulfillment references if possible)._____

    a._____

    b._____

8. What basic principle was God teaching?_____

©1973, John C. Souter. Not to be reproduced.

Prophecy Study — 15 min.

Passage Selected_____ Date_____

1. Which prophet is speaking?_____
2. Who is he speaking to?_____
3. Why was the prophecy given?_____

4. How did the people of that day respond?_____

5. What immediate event does the prophecy foretell?_____

6. Is there a second (long range) prophecy given?_____

7. Explain how each prophecy has been fulfilled. (Give fulfillment references if possible)._____
   a._____

   b._____

8. What basic principle was God teaching?_____

©1973, John C. Souter. Not to be reproduced.

Prophecy Study 15 min.

Passage Selected_____ Date_____

1. Which prophet is speaking?_____
2. Who is he speaking to?_____
3. Why was the prophecy given?_____
_____
_____

4. How did the people of that day respond?_____
_____
_____

5. What immediate event does the prophecy foretell?_____
_____
_____
_____

6. Is there a second (long range) prophecy given?_____
_____
_____
_____

7. Explain how each prophecy has been fulfilled. (Give fulfillment references if possible)._____
    a._____
_____
_____
    b._____
_____
_____

8. What basic principle was God teaching?_____
_____
_____
_____

©1973, John C. Souter. Not to be reproduced.

Epistle Study 15 min.

Passage Selected _____ Date _____

1. Check the type of passage: _____
   ☐ Doctrinal ☐ Instructional ☐ Personal ☐ Correctional
2. Does the author give any personal information? _____
   _____
   _____

3. What exhortations or commands are given? _____
   _____
   _____

4. What good qualities are encouraged? _____
   _____
   _____

5. What problem needed correction? _____
   _____
   _____

6. What light does the context throw on the passage? _____
   _____
   _____

7. What basic doctrinal truths are taught? _____
   _____
   _____

8. What underlying principle does God want me to learn? _____
   _____
   _____

©1973, John C. Souter. Not to be reproduced.

Epistle Study · 15 min.

Passage Selected _____ Date _____

1. Check the type of passage: _____ _____
   ☐ Doctrinal ☐ Instructional ☐ Personal ☐ Correctional

2. Does the author give any personal information? _____
   _____
   _____

3. What exhortations or commands are given? _____
   _____
   _____

4. What good qualities are encouraged? _____
   _____
   _____

5. What problem needed correction? _____
   _____
   _____

6. What light does the context throw on the passage? _____
   _____

7. What basic doctrinal truths are taught? _____
   _____
   _____

8. What underlying principle does God want me to learn? _____
   _____
   _____

Epistle Study — 15 min.

Passage Selected _____ Date _____

1. Check the type of passage: _____
   ☐ Doctrinal   ☐ Instructional   ☐ Personal   ☐ Correctional
2. Does the author give any personal information? _____
   _____
   _____

3. What exhortations or commands are given? _____
   _____
   _____

4. What good qualities are encouraged? _____
   _____
   _____

5. What problem needed correction? _____
   _____
   _____

6. What light does the context throw on the passage? _____
   _____
   _____

7. What basic doctrinal truths are taught? _____
   _____
   _____

8. What underlying principle does God want me to learn? _____
   _____
   _____

© 1973, John C. Souter. Not to be reproduced.

Epistle Study — 15 min.

Passage Selected_____ Date_____

1. Check the type of passage:_____
   ☐ Doctrinal ☐ Instructional ☐ Personal ☐ Correctional
2. Does the author give any personal information?_____
   _____
   _____

3. What exhortations or commands are given?_____
   _____
   _____
   _____

4. What good qualities are encouraged?_____
   _____
   _____
   _____

5. What problem needed correction?_____
   _____
   _____
   _____

6. What light does the context throw on the passage?_____
   _____
   _____

7. What basic doctrinal truths are taught?_____
   _____
   _____
   _____

8. What underlying principle does God want me to learn?____
   _____
   _____
   _____

Epistle Study 15 min.

Passage Selected _____ Date _____

1. Check the type of passage: _____
   ☐ Doctrinal ☐ Instructional ☐ Personal ☐ Correctional
2. Does the author give any personal information? _____
   _____
   _____

3. What exhortations or commands are given? _____
   _____
   _____

4. What good qualities are encouraged? _____
   _____
   _____

5. What problem needed correction? _____
   _____
   _____

6. What light does the context throw on the passage? ___
   _____

7. What basic doctrinal truths are taught? _____
   _____
   _____

8. What underlying principle does God want me to learn? ___
   _____
   _____

© 1973, John C. Souter. Not to be reproduced.

Epistle Study — 15 min.

Passage Selected _____ Date _____

1. Check the type of passage: _____
   ☐ Doctrinal   ☐ Instructional   ☐ Personal   ☐ Correctional
2. Does the author give any personal information? _____
   _____
   _____

3. What exhortations or commands are given? _____
   _____
   _____
   _____

4. What good qualities are encouraged? _____
   _____
   _____
   _____

5. What problem needed correction? _____
   _____
   _____
   _____

6. What light does the context throw on the passage? _____
   _____
   _____

7. What basic doctrinal truths are taught? _____
   _____
   _____
   _____

8. What underlying principle does God want me to learn? _____
   _____
   _____
   _____

© 1973, John C. Souter. Not to be reproduced.

Epistle Study 15 min.

Passage Selected_____ Date_____

1. Check the type of passage:_____
   ☐ Doctrinal ☐ Instructional ☐ Personal ☐ Correctional
2. Does the author give any personal information?_____
   _____
   _____

3. What exhortations or commands are given?_____
   _____
   _____
   _____

4. What good qualities are encouraged?_____
   _____
   _____
   _____

5. What problem needed correction?_____
   _____
   _____
   _____

6. What light does the context throw on the passage?___
   _____
   _____
   _____

7. What basic doctrinal truths are taught?_____
   _____
   _____
   _____

8. What underlying principle does God want me to learn?___
   _____
   _____
   _____

©1973, John C. Souter. Not to be reproduced.

Epistle Study　　15 min.

Passage Selected_____ Date_____

1. Check the type of passage:_____ _____
   ☐ Doctrinal   ☐ Instructional   ☐ Personal   ☐ Correctional
2. Does the author give any personal information?_____
   _____
   _____

3. What exhortations or commands are given?_____
   _____
   _____
   _____

4. What good qualities are encouraged?_____
   _____
   _____
   _____

5. What problem needed correction?_____
   _____
   _____
   _____

6. What light does the context throw on the passage?_____
   _____
   _____

7. What basic doctrinal truths are taught?_____
   _____
   _____
   _____

8. What underlying principle does God want me to learn?_____
   _____
   _____
   _____

©1973, John C. Souter. Not to be reproduced.

Epistle Study　　　15 min.

Passage Selected_____ Date_____

1. Check the type of passage:_____
   ☐ Doctrinal　☐ Instructional　☐ Personal　☐ Correctional

2. Does the author give any personal information?_____
   _____
   _____

3. What exhortations or commands are given?_____
   _____
   _____

4. What good qualities are encouraged?_____
   _____
   _____

5. What problem needed correction?_____
   _____
   _____

6. What light does the context throw on the passage?_____
   _____
   _____

7. What basic doctrinal truths are taught?_____
   _____
   _____

8. What underlying principle does God want me to learn?__
   _____
   _____

© 1973, John C. Souter. Not to be reproduced.

Epistle Study — 15 min.

Passage Selected _____ Date _____

1. Check the type of passage: _____
   - ☐ Doctrinal ☐ Instructional ☐ Personal ☐ Correctional
2. Does the author give any personal information? _____
   _____
   _____

3. What exhortations or commands are given? _____
   _____
   _____
   _____

4. What good qualities are encouraged? _____
   _____
   _____
   _____

5. What problem needed correction? _____
   _____
   _____
   _____

6. What light does the context throw on the passage? _____
   _____
   _____

7. What basic doctrinal truths are taught? _____
   _____
   _____
   _____

8. What underlying principle does God want me to learn? _____
   _____
   _____
   _____

©1973, John C. Souter. Not to be reproduced.

The Five W's — 15 min.

Passage Selected_____ Date_____

1. Skim the passage.
2. WHO is involved?_____
_____
3. WHEN did this event take place?_____
   a. Approximate date:_____
   b. Day of week:_____
   c. Hour of day:_____
   d. Relationship to some other event:_____
_____
4. WHERE did the action take place?_____
   a. Country:_____
   b. Province:_____
   c. City:_____
   d. Geography:_____
   e. Building:_____
5. WHAT took place?_____
_____
_____
_____
_____
6. WHY did this event take place?_____
_____
_____
_____
7. What is God teaching me in this passage?_____
_____
_____

© 1973, John C. Souter. Not to be reproduced.

The Five W's 15 min.

Passage Selected_____ Date_____

1. Skim the passage.
2. WHO is involved?_____
   _____
3. WHEN did this event take place?_____
   a. Approximate date:_____
   b. Day of week:_____
   c. Hour of day:_____
   d. Relationship to some other event:____
   _____
4. WHERE did the action take place?_____
   a. Country:_____
   b. Province:_____
   c. City:_____
   d. Geography:_____
   e. Building:_____
5. WHAT took place?_____
   _____
   _____
   _____
   _____
   _____
6. WHY did this event take place?_____
   _____
   _____
   _____
7. What is God teaching me in this passage?___
   _____
   _____

© 1973, John C. Souter. Not to be reproduced.

The Five W's   15 min.

Passage Selected_____ Date_____

1. Skim the passage.
2. WHO is involved?_____
   _____
3. WHEN did this event take place?_____
   a. Approximate date:_____
   b. Day of week:_____
   c. Hour of day:_____
   d. Relationship to some other event:_____
   _____
4. WHERE did the action take place?_____
   a. Country:_____
   b. Province:_____
   c. City:_____
   d. Geography:_____
   e. Building:_____
5. WHAT took place?_____
   _____
   _____
   _____
   _____
6. WHY did this event take place?_____
   _____
   _____
   _____
7. What is God teaching me in this passage?_____
   _____
   _____

© 1973, John C. Souter. Not to be reproduced.

The Five W's   15 min.

Passage Selected_____Date_____

1. Skim the passage.
2. WHO is involved?_____
   _____
3. WHEN did this event take place?_____
   a. Approximate date:_____
   b. Day of week:_____
   c. Hour of day:_____
   d. Relationship to some other event:_____
   _____
4. WHERE did the action take place?_____
   a. Country:_____
   b. Province:_____
   c. City:_____
   d. Geography:_____
   e. Building:_____
5. WHAT took place?_____
   _____
   _____
   _____
   _____
6. WHY did this event take place?_____
   _____
   _____
7. What is God teaching me in this passage?_____
   _____
   _____

©1973, John C. Souter. Not to be reproduced.

The Five W's   15 min.

Passage Selected_____ Date_____

1. Skim the passage.
2. WHO is involved?_____
   _____
3. WHEN did this event take place?_____
   a. Approximate date:_____
   b. Day of week:_____
   c. Hour of day:_____
   d. Relationship to some other event:_____
   _____
4. WHERE did the action take place?_____
   a. Country:_____
   b. Province:_____
   c. City:_____
   d. Geography:_____
   e. Building:_____
5. WHAT took place?_____
   _____
   _____
   _____
   _____
6. WHY did this event take place?_____
   _____
   _____
   _____
7. What is God teaching me in this passage?_____
   _____
   _____
   _____

© 1973, John C. Souter. Not to be reproduced.

The Five W's 15 min.

Passage Selected_____Date_____

1. Skim the passage.
2. WHO is involved?_____
   _____
3. WHEN did this event take place?_____
   a. Approximate date:_____
   b. Day of week:_____
   c. Hour of day:_____
   d. Relationship to some other event:_____
   _____
4. WHERE did the action take place?_____
   a. Country:_____
   b. Province:_____
   c. City:_____
   d. Geography:_____
   e. Building:_____
5. WHAT took place?_____
   _____
   _____
   _____
   _____
6. WHY did this event take place?_____
   _____
   _____
   _____
7. What is God teaching me in this passage?_____
   _____
   _____
   _____

©1973, John C. Souter. Not to be reproduced.

The Five W's 15 min.

Passage Selected_____ Date_____

1. Skim the passage.
2. WHO is involved?_____
   _____
3. WHEN did this event take place?_____
   a. Approximate date:_____
   b. Day of week:_____
   c. Hour of day:_____
   d. Relationship to some other event:_____
   _____
4. WHERE did the action take place?_____
   a. Country:_____
   b. Province:_____
   c. City:_____
   d. Geography:_____
   e. Building:_____
5. WHAT took place?_____
   _____
   _____
   _____
   _____
6. WHY did this event take place?_____
   _____
   _____
   _____
7. What is God teaching me in this passage?_____
   _____
   _____

©1973, John C. Souter. Not to be reproduced.

The Five W's 15 min.

Passage Selected_____Date_____

1. Skim the passage.
2. WHO is involved?_____
   _____
3. WHEN did this event take place?_____
   a. Approximate date:_____
   b. Day of week:_____
   c. Hour of day:_____
   d. Relationship to some other event:_____
   _____
4. WHERE did the action take place?_____
   a. Country:_____
   b. Province:_____
   c. City:_____
   d. Geography:_____
   e. Building:_____
5. WHAT took place?_____
   _____
   _____
   _____
   _____
   _____
6. WHY did this event take place?_____
   _____
   _____
   _____
7. What is God teaching me in this passage?_____
   _____
   _____
   _____

©1973, John C. Souter. Not to be reproduced.

The Five W's 15 min.

Passage Selected_____Date_____

1. Skim the passage.
2. WHO is involved?_____
   _____
3. WHEN did this event take place?_____
   a. Approximate date:_____
   b. Day of week:_____
   c. Hour of day:_____
   d. Relationship to some other event:_____
   _____
4. WHERE did the action take place?_____
   a. Country:_____
   b. Province:_____
   c. City:_____
   d. Geography:_____
   e. Building:_____
5. WHAT took place?_____
   _____
   _____
   _____
   _____
6. WHY did this event take place?_____
   _____
   _____
   _____
7. What is God teaching me in this passage?_____
   _____
   _____

© 1973, John C. Souter. Not to be reproduced.

The Five W's 15 min.

Passage Selected_____Date_____

1. Skim the passage.
2. WHO is involved?_____

_____

3. WHEN did this event take place?_____
   a. Approximate date:_____
   b. Day of week:_____
   c. Hour of day:_____
   d. Relationship to some other event:_____

_____

4. WHERE did the action take place?_____
   a. Country:_____
   b. Province:_____
   c. City:_____
   d. Geography:_____
   e. Building:_____
5. WHAT took place?_____

_____

_____

_____

_____

6. WHY did this event take place?_____

_____

_____

7. What is God teaching me in this passage?_____

_____

_____

©1973, John C. Souter. Not to be reproduced.

Teachings of Jesus　　15 min.

Passage Selected_____ Date_____

1. What parable or story is told?_____

Summarize it:_____

_____

_____

_____

2. What interpretation does Jesus give?_____

_____

_____

_____

3. Does He quote from the Old Testament?_____

What?_____

_____

4. What does Jesus condemn?_____

Why?_____

_____

_____

5. What good qualities does He encourage?_____

_____

_____

_____

6. What is the basic underlying principle He is teaching?____

_____

_____

_____

7. How can I apply these teachings?_____

_____

_____

_____

© 1973, John C. Souter. Not to be reproduced.

Teachings of Jesus   15 min.

Passage Selected_____ Date_____

1. What parable or story is told?_____

Summarize it:_____
_____
_____
_____

2. What interpretation does Jesus give?_____
_____
_____

3. Does He quote from the Old Testament?_____
What?_____
_____

4. What does Jesus condemn?_____
Why?_____
_____

5. What good qualities does He encourage?_____
_____
_____

6. What is the basic underlying principle He is teaching?_____
_____
_____

7. How can I apply these teachings?_____
_____
_____

©1973, John C. Souter. Not to be reproduced.

Teachings of Jesus   15 min.

Passage Selected_____ Date_____

1. What parable or story is told?_____
Summarize it:_____
_____
_____
_____

2. What interpretation does Jesus give?_____
_____
_____

3. Does He quote from the Old Testament?_____
What?_____
_____

4. What does Jesus condemn?_____
Why?_____
_____

5. What good qualities does He encourage?_____
_____
_____

6. What is the basic underlying principle He is teaching?_____
_____
_____
_____

7. How can I apply these teachings?_____
_____
_____
_____

© 1973, John C. Souter. Not to be reproduced.

Teachings of Jesus   15 min.

Passage Selected_____ Date_____

1. What parable or story is told?_____
Summarize it:_____
_____
_____
_____

2. What interpretation does Jesus give?_____
_____
_____

3. Does He quote from the Old Testament?_____
What?_____
_____

4. What does Jesus condemn?_____
Why?_____
_____
_____

5. What good qualities does He encourage?_____
_____
_____
_____

6. What is the basic underlying principle He is teaching?_____
_____
_____
_____

7. How can I apply these teachings?_____
_____
_____
_____

©1973, John C. Souter. Not to be reproduced.

Teachings of Jesus — 15 min.

Passage Selected_____ Date_____

1. What parable or story is told?_____

Summarize it:_____

_____

_____

_____

2. What interpretation does Jesus give?_____

_____

_____

_____

3. Does He quote from the Old Testament?_____

What?_____

_____

4. What does Jesus condemn?_____

Why?_____

_____

5. What good qualities does He encourage?_____

_____

_____

_____

6. What is the basic underlying principle He is teaching?_____

_____

_____

_____

7. How can I apply these teachings?_____

_____

_____

_____

©1973, John C. Souter. Not to be reproduced.

Teachings of Jesus　　15 min.

Passage Selected_____Date_____

1. What parable or story is told?_____

Summarize it:_____

_____

_____

_____

2. What interpretation does Jesus give?_____

_____

_____

_____

3. Does He quote from the Old Testament?_____

What?_____

_____

4. What does Jesus condemn?_____

Why?_____

_____

_____

5. What good qualities does He encourage?_____

_____

_____

_____

6. What is the basic underlying principle He is teaching?_____

_____

_____

_____

7. How can I apply these teachings?_____

_____

_____

_____

©1973, John C. Souter. Not to be reproduced.

Teachings of Jesus   15 min.

Passage Selected_____ Date_____

1. What parable or story is told?_____
Summarize it:_____
_____
_____

2. What interpretation does Jesus give?_____
_____
_____

3. Does He quote from the Old Testament?_____
What?_____
_____

4. What does Jesus condemn?_____
Why?_____
_____

5. What good qualities does He encourage?_____
_____
_____

6. What is the basic underlying principle He is teaching?_____
_____
_____

7. How can I apply these teachings?_____
_____
_____

©1973, John C. Souter. Not to be reproduced.

Teachings of Jesus   15 min.

Passage Selected_____ Date_____

1. What parable or story is told?_____

Summarize it:_____

_____

_____

_____

2. What interpretation does Jesus give?_____

_____

_____

3. Does He quote from the Old Testament?_____

What?_____

_____

4. What does Jesus condemn?_____

Why?_____

_____

5. What good qualities does He encourage?_____

_____

_____

6. What is the basic underlying principle He is teaching?___

_____

_____

7. How can I apply these teachings?_____

_____

_____

©1973, John C. Souter. Not to be reproduced.

Teachings of Jesus   15 min.

Passage Selected_____ Date_____

1. What parable or story is told?_____
Summarize it:_____
_____
_____
_____

2. What interpretation does Jesus give?_____
_____
_____
_____

3. Does He quote from the Old Testament?_____
What?_____
_____

4. What does Jesus condemn?_____
Why?_____
_____
_____

5. What good qualities does He encourage?_____
_____
_____
_____

6. What is the basic underlying principle He is teaching?_____
_____
_____
_____

7. How can I apply these teachings?_____
_____
_____
_____

©1973, John C. Souter. Not to be reproduced.

Teachings of Jesus   15 min.

Passage Selected_____Date_____

1. What parable or story is told?_____

Summarize it:_____
_____
_____
_____

2. What interpretation does Jesus give?_____
_____
_____
_____

3. Does He quote from the Old Testament?_____
What?_____
_____

4. What does Jesus condemn?_____
Why?_____
_____
_____

5. What good qualities does He encourage?_____
_____
_____
_____

6. What is the basic underlying principle He is teaching?____
_____
_____
_____

7. How can I apply these teachings?_____
_____
_____
_____

168   © 1973, John C. Souter. Not to be reproduced.

Biography Study — 30 min.

Character Selected _____ Date _____

1. List the passages on this person: _____
   _____
   _____

2. Skim above passages.

HISTORY

Write the major facts of his life in chronological order:

1. His introduction: _____
   _____
   _____
   _____

2. General life: _____
   _____
   _____
   _____

3. Great accomplishments: _____
   _____
   _____
   _____

4. Relationship with God: _____
   _____
   _____
   _____

5. How last mentioned (death): _____
   _____
   _____

6. One sentence summary of life: _____
   _____
   _____

© 1973, John C. Souter. Not to be reproduced.

BACKGROUND

1. Meaning of his name: _____

2. His training: _____

3. His race, tribe & parents: _____

4. His ancestors or descendants: _____

5. His occupation: _____

CHARACTER

1. His faults: _____

2. His good qualities: _____

3. His attitude toward God: _____

APPLICATION

1. Why did God put him in the Bible? _____

2. Did I see any of myself in his life? _____

3. What did his life teach me? _____

Biography Study — 30 min.

Character Selected _____ Date _____

1. List the passages on this person: _____
   _____
   _____

2. Skim above passages.

HISTORY

Write the major facts of his life in chronological order:

1. His introduction: _____
   _____
   _____
   _____

2. General life: _____
   _____
   _____
   _____

3. Great accomplishments: _____
   _____
   _____
   _____

4. Relationship with God: _____
   _____
   _____
   _____

5. How last mentioned (death): _____
   _____
   _____

6. One sentence summary of life: _____
   _____

©1973, John C. Souter. Not to be reproduced.

BACKGROUND

1. Meaning of his name: _____
   _____

2. His training: _____
   _____

3. His race, tribe & parents: _____
   _____

4. His ancestors or descendants: _____
   _____

5. His occupation: _____
   _____

CHARACTER

1. His faults: _____
   _____
   _____

2. His good qualities: _____
   _____
   _____

3. His attitude toward God: _____
   _____
   _____

APPLICATION

1. Why did God put him in the Bible? _____
   _____

2. Did I see any of myself in his life? _____
   _____

3. What did his life teach me? _____
   _____

Biography Study — 30 min.

Character Selected _____ Date _____

1. List the passages on this person: _____
   _____
   _____

2. Skim above passages.

HISTORY

Write the major facts of his life in chronological order:

1. His introduction: _____
   _____
   _____
   _____

2. General life: _____
   _____
   _____
   _____

3. Great accomplishments: _____
   _____
   _____
   _____

4. Relationship with God: _____
   _____
   _____
   _____

5. How last mentioned (death): _____
   _____
   _____

6. One sentence summary of life: _____
   _____
   _____

© 1973, John C. Souter. Not to be reproduced.

BACKGROUND

1. Meaning of his name: _____

2. His training: _____

3. His race, tribe & parents: _____

4. His ancestors or descendants: _____

5. His occupation: _____

CHARACTER

1. His faults: _____

2. His good qualities: _____

3. His attitude toward God: _____

APPLICATION

1. Why did God put him in the Bible? _____

2. Did I see any of myself in his life? _____

3. What did his life teach me? _____

Biography Study 30 min.

Character Selected _____ Date _____

1. List the passages on this person: _____

_____

_____

2. Skim above passages.

HISTORY

Write the major facts of his life in chronological order:

1. His introduction: _____

_____

_____

_____

2. General life: _____

_____

_____

_____

3. Great accomplishments: _____

_____

_____

_____

4. Relationship with God: _____

_____

_____

_____

5. How last mentioned (death): _____

_____

_____

6. One sentence summary of life: _____

_____

© 1973, John C. Souter. Not to be reproduced.

BACKGROUND

1. Meaning of his name: _____

2. His training: _____

3. His race, tribe & parents: _____

4. His ancestors or descendants: _____

5. His occupation: _____

CHARACTER

1. His faults: _____

2. His good qualities: _____

3. His attitude toward God: _____

APPLICATION

1. Why did God put him in the Bible? _____

2. Did I see any of myself in his life? _____

3. What did his life teach me? _____

Biography Study 30 min.

Character Selected_____ Date_____

1. List the passages on this person:_____
_____
_____

2. Skim above passages.

HISTORY

Write the major facts of his life in chronological order:

1. His introduction:_____
_____
_____
_____

2. General life:_____
_____
_____
_____

3. Great accomplishments:_____
_____
_____
_____

4. Relationship with God:_____
_____
_____
_____

5. How last mentioned (death):_____
_____
_____

6. One sentence summary of life:_____
_____

© 1973, John C. Souter. Not to be reproduced.

BACKGROUND

1. Meaning of his name:

2. His training:

3. His race, tribe & parents:

4. His ancestors or descendants:

5. His occupation:

CHARACTER

1. His faults:

2. His good qualities:

3. His attitude toward God:

APPLICATION

1. Why did God put him in the Bible?

2. Did I see any of myself in his life?

3. What did his life teach me?

Book Study 30 min.

Book Selected_____ Date_____

BACKGROUND
1. Who is the writer?_____
   a. His occupation?_____
   b. Approximate age?_____
   c. Personality traits?_____
   _____
   _____

2. Where was the book written?_____
3. Where was it sent?_____
4. When was it written?_____
5. Why was it written?_____
   _____

THEME
1. Key thought?_____
   _____
2. Key verse?_____
3. Summary of book contents:_____
   _____
   _____

SPECIAL CHARACTERISTICS
1. What words or phrases are peculiar to this book?_____
   _____
   _____

2. What are some of its important teachings?_____
   _____

©1973, John C. Souter. Not to be reproduced.

OUTLINE OF BOOK

Using a Bible Dictionary, copy the outline given for the entire book.

MAIN DIVISIONS	REFERENCES

APPLICATION

1. Does the problem for which this book was written apply to me? _____ If yes, what am I doing to correct it? _____

2. What subjects does this book deal with that I personally need? _____

3. What different study methods will I use to study this book in greater detail? _____

Book Study — 30 min.

Book Selected_____ Date_____

BACKGROUND

1. Who is the writer?_____
   a. His occupation?_____
   b. Approximate age?_____
   c. Personality traits?_____
   _____
   _____

2. Where was the book written?_____
3. Where was it sent?_____
4. When was it written?_____
5. Why was it written?_____
   _____
   _____

THEME

1. Key thought?_____
   _____
2. Key verse?_____
3. Summary of book contents:_____
   _____
   _____

SPECIAL CHARACTERISTICS

1. What words or phrases are peculiar to this book?_____
   _____
   _____
   _____

2. What are some of its important teachings?_____
   _____
   _____

© 1973, John C. Souter. Not to be reproduced.

OUTLINE OF BOOK

Using a Bible Dictionary, copy the outline given for the entire book.

MAIN DIVISIONS	REFERENCES

APPLICATION

1. Does the problem for which this book was written apply to me? _____ If yes, what am I doing to correct it? _____

2. What subjects does this book deal with that I personally need? _____

3. What different study methods will I use to study this book in greater detail? _____

Book Study 30 min.

Book Selected_____ Date_____

BACKGROUND
1. Who is the writer?_____
   a. His occupation?_____
   b. Approximate age?_____
   c. Personality traits?_____
   _____
   _____

2. Where was the book written?_____
3. Where was it sent?_____
4. When was it written?_____
5. Why was it written?_____
   _____
   _____

THEME
1. Key thought?_____
   _____
2. Key verse?_____
3. Summary of book contents:_____
   _____
   _____

SPECIAL CHARACTERISTICS
1. What words or phrases are peculiar to this book?_____
   _____
   _____
   _____

2. What are some of its important teachings?_____
   _____

© 1973, John C. Souter. Not to be reproduced.

OUTLINE OF BOOK

Using a Bible Dictionary, copy the outline given for the entire book.

MAIN DIVISIONS	REFERENCES

APPLICATION

1. Does the problem for which this book was written apply to me? _____ If yes, what am I doing to correct it? _____

2. What subjects does this book deal with that I personally need? _____

3. What different study methods will I use to study this book in greater detail? _____

Book Study — 30 min.

Book Selected_____ Date_____

BACKGROUND

1. Who is the writer?_____
   a. His occupation?_____
   b. Approximate age?_____
   c. Personality traits?_____
   _____
   _____

2. Where was the book written?_____
3. Where was it sent?_____
4. When was it written?_____
5. Why was it written?_____
   _____
   _____

THEME

1. Key thought?_____
   _____

2. Key verse?_____
3. Summary of book contents:_____
   _____
   _____

SPECIAL CHARACTERISTICS

1. What words or phrases are peculiar to this book?_____
   _____
   _____
   _____

2. What are some of its important teachings?_____
   _____
   _____

OUTLINE OF BOOK

Using a Bible Dictionary, copy the outline given for the entire book.

MAIN DIVISIONS	REFERENCES

APPLICATION

1. Does the problem for which this book was written apply to me? _____ If yes, what am I doing to correct it? _____

2. What subjects does this book deal with that I personally need? _____

3. What different study methods will I use to study this book in greater detail? _____

Book Study — 30 min.

Book Selected_____ Date_____

BACKGROUND

1. Who is the writer?_____
   a. His occupation?_____
   b. Approximate age?_____
   c. Personality traits?_____
   _____
   _____

2. Where was the book written?_____
3. Where was it sent?_____
4. When was it written?_____
5. Why was it written?_____
   _____
   _____

THEME

1. Key thought?_____
   _____
2. Key verse?_____
3. Summary of book contents:_____
   _____
   _____

SPECIAL CHARACTERISTICS

1. What words or phrases are peculiar to this book?_____
   _____
   _____
   _____

2. What are some of its important teachings?_____
   _____
   _____

©1973, John C. Souter. Not to be reproduced.

OUTLINE OF BOOK

Using a Bible Dictionary, copy the outline given for the entire book.

MAIN DIVISIONS	REFERENCES

APPLICATION

1. Does the problem for which this book was written apply to me? _____ If yes, what am I doing to correct it? _____

2. What subjects does this book deal with that I personally need? _____

3. What different study methods will I use to study this book in greater detail? _____